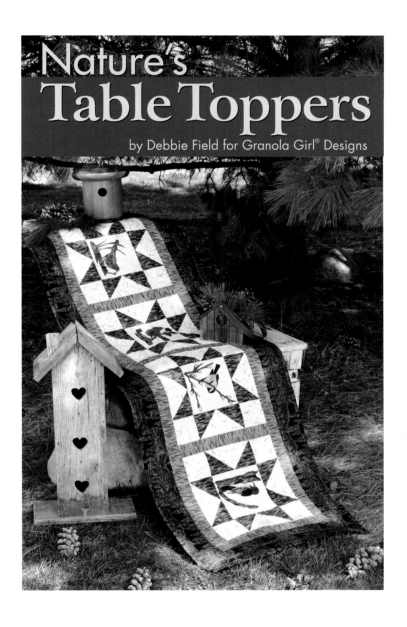

Nature's
Table Toppers

by Debbie Field for Granola Girl® Designs

Landauer Publishing, LLC

Nature's Table Toppers
by Debbie Field for Granola Girl® Designs

Copyright © 2011 by Landauer Publishing, LLC
Projects & Patterns Copyright © 2011 by Debbie Field

This book was designed, produced, and published by Landauer Publishing, LLC
3100 101st Street, Urbandale, IA 50322
515-287-2144; 800-557-2144; www.landauercorp.com

President/Publisher: Jeramy Lanigan Landauer
Vice President of Sales & Administration: Kitty Jacobson
Editor: Jeri Simon
Art Director: Laurel Albright
Technical Illustrator: Linda Bender
Photography: Sue Voegtlin

Library of Congress Control Number: 2011929085
ISBN 13: 978-1-935726-10-4
ISBN 10: 1-935726-10-2

This book is printed on acid-free paper.
Printed in China by C&C Offset Printing Co., Ltd.
10 9 8 7 6 5 4 3 2 1

introduction

Celebrate nature throughout the year with the outdoor-inspired projects in this book. You'll discover new home decorating projects with designs featuring birds, pumpkins, wildflowers, and my signature Northwoods theme.

Projects range from a bright, summer dragonfly table runner to a rustic, round wool table topper to a high-flying witch and black cat—something for everyone.

All 20 table toppers are quick-to-complete with clear, step-by-step instructions and appliqué patterns. Cotton was used in some of the projects and wool in others. Feel free to mix it up and create nature-inspired table toppers for every season. Take time for quilting and enjoy the outdoors.

Debbie Field

A special thank you to my creative team for your individual talents.

Delores Farmer
Sue Carter
Jennifer Bauer
Cindy Kujawa

Forever true,
forever
friends.

Contents

Contents

Contents

general instructions

Assemble the tools and supplies to complete the project. In addition to basic cutting and sewing tools, the following will make cutting and sewing easier: small sharp scissors to cut appliqué shapes, rotary cutter and mat, extra rotary blades, and a transparent ruler with markings.

Replace the sewing machine needle each time you start a project to maintain even stitches and to prevent skipped stitches and broken needles during the project. Clean the machine after every project to remove lint and to keep it running smoothly.

The projects shown are made with unwashed fabrics. If you prewash fabrics, purchase extra yardage to allow for shrinkage. The 100-percent cottons and flannels used in the wilderness quilts and accessories are from Debbie's Granola Girl® collections: Marblecake Basics, Sport Fishing, Gone Fishing, and Pheasant and Turkey Season fabric lines manufactured by Troy Corporation. Ask for them by name at your local quilt shop.

Please read through the project instructions before cutting and sewing. Square the fabric before cutting by placing the folded fabric on your cutting mat. Align one of the horizontal lines on the ruler with the folded edge nearest you. Place your rotary cutter at the right edge of your ruler and cut fabric from selvage to selvage. Square your fabric again after cutting 3 or 4 strips.

To create accurate half-square triangles, align your ruler diagonally from corner to corner on each fabric square and cut.

Sew with 1/4" seam allowances throughout, unless stated otherwise in the instructions, and check seam allowance accuracy to prevent compounding even slight errors. Press seams toward the darker fabric when possible. When pressing small joined pieces, press in the direction that creates less bulk.

basic appliqué

Please note that the printed appliqué templates are reversed. Trace and cut the templates as printed, unless the illustrations and photos indicate to reverse the templates. For appliqués that face the opposite direction, trace and reverse the template. Dashed lines indicate design's overlay or, if stated, embellishment.

Trace the appliqué template to the fusible webbing with a fine tip marker or sharp pencil, allowing space to cut 1/4" beyond the traced lines. Position the fusible web on the wrong side of the appliqué fabric. Follow the manufacturer's instructions to fuse the webbing to the fabric. Allow the fabric to cool and cut along the traced line. Remove paper backing and follow the photographs and layout diagrams to position the appliqué pieces on the background fabrics.

Use lightweight tear-away stabilizer to machine appliqué. Place the stabilizer beneath the fabric layers and use a small, zigzag stitch to sew around each shape, smoothly covering the raw fabric edge. The stitch is meant to secure the outermost edge of an appliqué shape in place. Your stitches should lie close together without appearing bunched up. If your machine has stitch options, use them to detail appliqués. After the stitching is complete, remove the stabilizer according to the manufacturer's instructions.

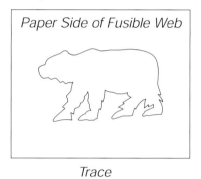

Paper Side of Fusible Web

Trace

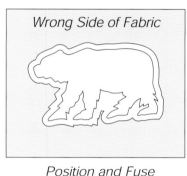

Wrong Side of Fabric

Position and Fuse

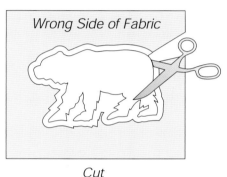

Wrong Side of Fabric

Cut

Peel

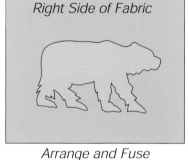

Right Side of Fabric

Arrange and Fuse

wool hints

Pre-washed, hand-dyed wools were used for the projects in this book. All measurements are for felted wool.

Heat'n Bond® Lite was the fusible web used for the appliqué shapes. Use whatever works best for you.

Set your iron on the steam setting when fusing wool appliqués to the backgrounds. After all appliqués have been fused in place, turn the project over and lightly press again.

Valdani® size 12 pearl cotton thread was used in the book's projects. It is hand-dyed and 100 percent colorfast. Thread colors have been included in the materials lists.

A size 24 chenille needle was used to blanket stitch around the shapes and to finish the edges.

basic binding

1. Cut the binding strips for your project from selvage to selvage. Join them for a continuous length by sewing the short ends of the binding strips, right sides together, with diagonal seams. Trim 1/4" from the sewn line and press open, as shown. Fold the strip in half lengthwise, wrong sides together, and press.

2. Match the raw edges of the folded strip to the quilt top, along an edge and approximately 6" from a corner, allowing approximately 6" free to join to the opposite end of the binding. Avoid placing binding seams on corners. Sew the binding to the quilt top with a 1/4" seam allowance.

3. At the first corner, stop 1/4" from the corner, backstitch, raise the presser foot and needle, and rotate the quilt 90 degrees. Fold the binding back onto itself to create a miter.

4. Fold it along the adjacent seam, matching raw edges. Continue sewing to the next corner and repeat the mitered corner process.

5. Where the binding ends meet, fold under one binding edge 1/4", encase the opposite binding edge, and stitch it to the quilt top.

6. Trim the batting and backing fabric even with the quilt top and binding. Fold the binding strip to the back of the quilt and handsew it in place with a blind stitch. Sign and date the quilt, including the recipient's name if it is a gift.

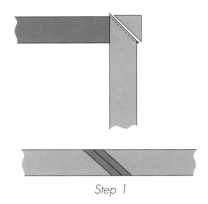

Step 1

Quilt — Binding Strip

Step 2

Quilt — Fold

Quilt

Step 3

Quilt — Start to sew at top of corner.

Step 4

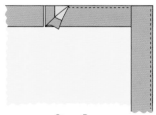

Step 5

basic quilting

- **Individual Motifs** Any design that stands alone, such as a flower or leaf, is a great choice for quilting the plain blocks in an alternating block quilt. You can often use a portion of an isolated motif to fill spaces in patchwork patterns. Designs along a border can also be repeated. Individual motifs can be square, circular, or oval—the range of possibilities is vast.

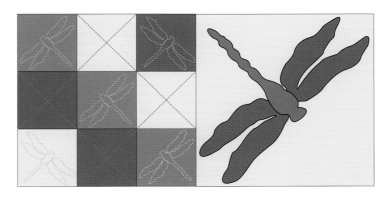

- **Stitching-in-the-Ditch** is stitching very close to the seams in a block. Patchwork blocks generally involve a lot of seam allowances. To avoid having to stitch through more layers than necessary with this type of block, try stitching-in-the-ditch along the side of the seam with the least amount of bulk.

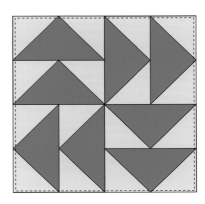

- **Outline Quilting** is a series of 1/4" stitching lines that outline the shape of the design in your block. You can choose to use this stitch to fill in the entire background section of your block.

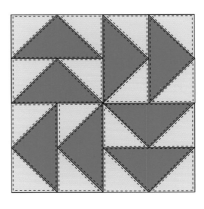

- **Meander or Stipple Quilting** has an overall pattern that resembles the curvy pieces of a jigsaw puzzle. Ideally the quilting lines don't touch or overlap one another. It is a nice choice for covering large areas quickly or adding texture behind an appliqué shape to make it stand out.

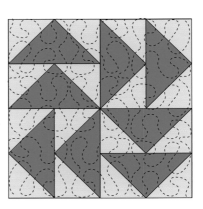

table runner
bird watching

Materials

Refer to the general instructions on pages 10-13 before starting this project.

1/2 yard of ecru twig fabric for star background

1/3 yard ecru woodgrain fabric for star center

1/3 yard olive woodgrain fabric for star triangles

3/8 yard gold woodgrain fabric for sashing and inner border

1-3/8 yards black background tree fabric for outer border and binding

1-3/4" x 5" piece of brown woodgrain fabric for robin back

2" x 3-1/2" piece of orange marblecake fabric for robin breast

2" x 2" square of gold marblecake fabric for robin beak and feet

1" x 2" piece of brown woodgrain fabric for worm

5" x 6" piece of olive green woodgrain fabric for grass

3-1/2" x 4-1/2" red marblecake fabric for cardinal body

1-1/2" x 3" dark red marblecake fabric for cardinal wing

1" x 1" piece of black marblecake fabric for cardinal face

1" x 1-1/2" piece of gray marblecake fabric for cardinal foot

1" x 1" square of gold marblecake fabric for cardinal beak

5" x 5" square of brown woodgrain fabric for branch

1-1/2" x 4" piece of dark green marblecake fabric for 3 leaves

1-1/2" x 1-1/2" square of medium green marblecake fabric for 1 leaf

2" x 3" piece of gray marblecake fabric for chickadee body

3" x 4" piece of black marblecake fabric for chickadee head, tail and feet

5" x 8" piece of brown woodgrain fabric for branches

2" x 5" piece of gray marblecake fabric for pussy willow buds

2" x 2" square of dark red marblecake for redheaded woodpecker head

2" x 3" piece of black marblecake fabric for redheaded woodpecker back and tail

1-1/2" x 3-1/2" piece of gray woodgrain fabric for redheaded woodpecker wing

2" x 3-1/2" piece of cream marblecake fabric for redheaded woodpecker breast

1" x 1-1/2" piece of black marblecake fabric for redheaded woodpecker foot

1" x 1-1/2" piece of gold marblecake fabric for redheaded woodpecker beak

3-1/2" x 6-1/2" piece of brown woodgrain fabric for tree trunk and branch

1-1/2" x 3-1/2" piece of black woodgrain fabric for inside tree trunk

2 yards of backing fabric

28" x 69" piece of batting

Lightweight paper-backed fusible web

Lightweight tear-away stabilizer

Sulky® threads to match appliqués

Note: Fabrics are based on 44"-wide fabrics that have not been washed. Please purchase accordingly if using prewashed or directional fabrics.

Instructions

Cutting

From ecru twig fabric:

Cut 1 strip — 7-1/4" x 44";
from strip cut 4 — 7-1/4" x 7-1/4" squares.
Cut squares in half diagonally twice to make
16 quarter-square triangles.

Cut 2 strips — 3-1/2" x 44";
from strips cut 16 — 3-1/2" x 3-1/2" squares.

From ecru woodgrain fabric:

Cut 1 strip — 6-1/2" x 44";
from strip cut 4 — 6-1/2" x 6-1/2" squares.

From olive woodgrain fabric:

Cut 2 strips — 3-7/8" x 44";
from strips cut 16 — 3-7/8" x 3-7/8" squares.
Cut squares in half diagonally to make
32 half-square triangles.

From gold woodgrain fabric:

Cut 5 strips — 2" x 44";
from 2 strips cut 5 — 2" x 12-1/2" rectangles.

From black background trees fabric:

Cut 1 strip — 17" x 44".
Cut 4 strips — 3-1/2" x 44".
Cut 5 strips — 2-3/4" x 44".

Block Assembly

1. Sew together an ecru twig 7-1/4" quarter-square triangle and an olive woodgrain 3-7/8" half-square triangle, as shown. Press the seam allowances toward the dark triangle. Repeat to make 16 Unit A.

Make 16 Unit A

2. Sew an olive woodgrain 3-7/8" half-square triangle to the opposite side of each Unit A, as shown to make 16 Unit B. Press the seam allowances toward the dark triangle.

Make 16 Unit B

3. Sew one Unit B to each side of the ecru woodgrain 6-1/2" squares to make 4 Unit C. Press the seam allowances toward the square.

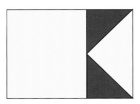

Make 4 Unit C

4. Sew one ecru twig 3-1/2" square to each end of each Unit B to make 8 Unit D. Press the seam allowances toward the squares.

Make 8 Unit D

5. Sew a Unit D to the top and bottom of a Unit C to make 4 Unit E. Press the seam allowances open.

Make 4 Unit E

Table Runner Top Assembly

Sew together 5 — 2" x 12-1/2" gold woodgrain sashing strips and 4 Unit E , as shown. Press the seam allowances toward the sashing strips.

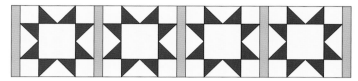

Borders

1. Measure the width of the table runner top through the center for the top and bottom border measurement. Use this measurement to cut 2 lengths from the 2"-wide gold woodgrain strips. Sew the lengths to the top and bottom edges of the table runner. Press the seam allowances toward the border.

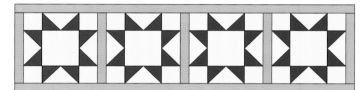

2. Measure the length of the runner top through the center to determine the side border measurement. Cut 2 rectangles 3-1/2" x length needed from the previously cut 17" x 44" black background trees strip. Sew to each side of the runner. Press the seam allowances toward the border.

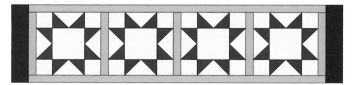

3. Measure the width of the runner top through the center for top and bottom border measurement. Use this measurement to cut 2 strips from the 3-1/2"-wide black background trees strips. Sew the strips to the top and bottom of the runner. Press the seam allowances toward the dark fabric.

Adding the Appliqués

1. Using the appliqué templates on pages 18-21, trace the shapes onto the paper side of the fusible web and cut out as directed.

2. Referring to Basic Appliqué instructions on page 10 and 11, prepare the fabric appliqué pieces. Referring to the layout guides on page 22, position the appliqués and fuse them in place.

3. Use a small zigzag stitch and matching thread to appliqué each shape to the runner. Remember to use tear-away stabilizer when stitching appliqués.

Finishing the Runner

Layer the backing fabric, batting and runner top. Baste the layers together. Hand or machine quilt as desired. Finish the runner by sewing binding to the edges, following the steps in Basic Binding on page 12.

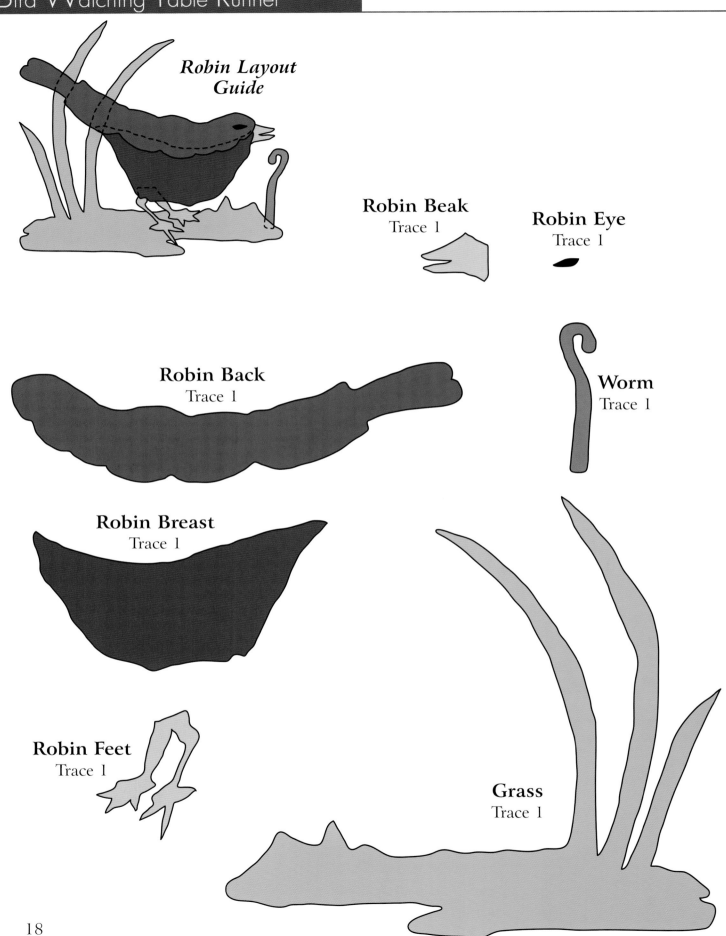

Robin Layout Guide

Robin Beak
Trace 1

Robin Eye
Trace 1

Robin Back
Trace 1

Worm
Trace 1

Robin Breast
Trace 1

Robin Feet
Trace 1

Grass
Trace 1

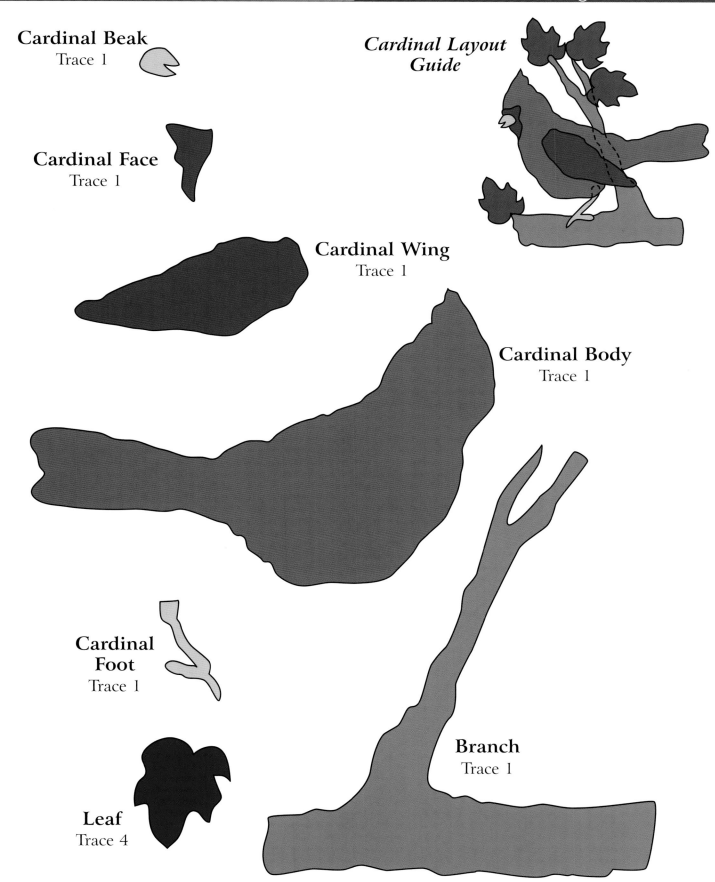

Cardinal Beak
Trace 1

Cardinal Layout Guide

Cardinal Face
Trace 1

Cardinal Wing
Trace 1

Cardinal Body
Trace 1

Cardinal Foot
Trace 1

Branch
Trace 1

Leaf
Trace 4

19

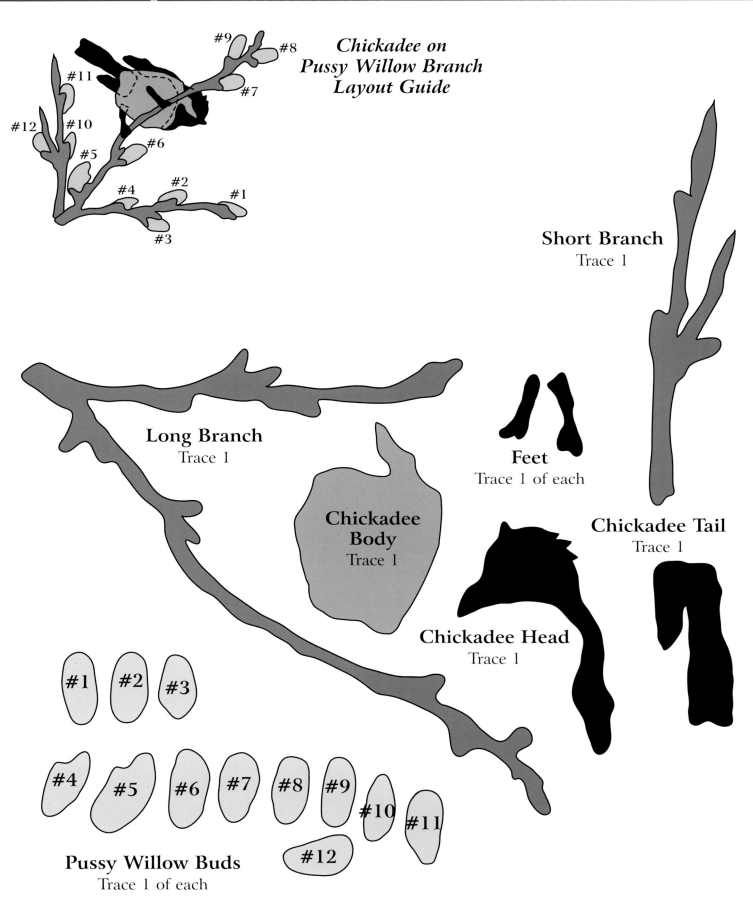

Chickadee on Pussy Willow Branch Layout Guide

#9 #8 #11 #7 #12 #10 #5 #6 #4 #2 #1 #3

Short Branch
Trace 1

Long Branch
Trace 1

Feet
Trace 1 of each

Chickadee Body
Trace 1

Chickadee Tail
Trace 1

Chickadee Head
Trace 1

#1 #2 #3

#4 #5 #6 #7 #8 #9 #10 #11 #12

Pussy Willow Buds
Trace 1 of each

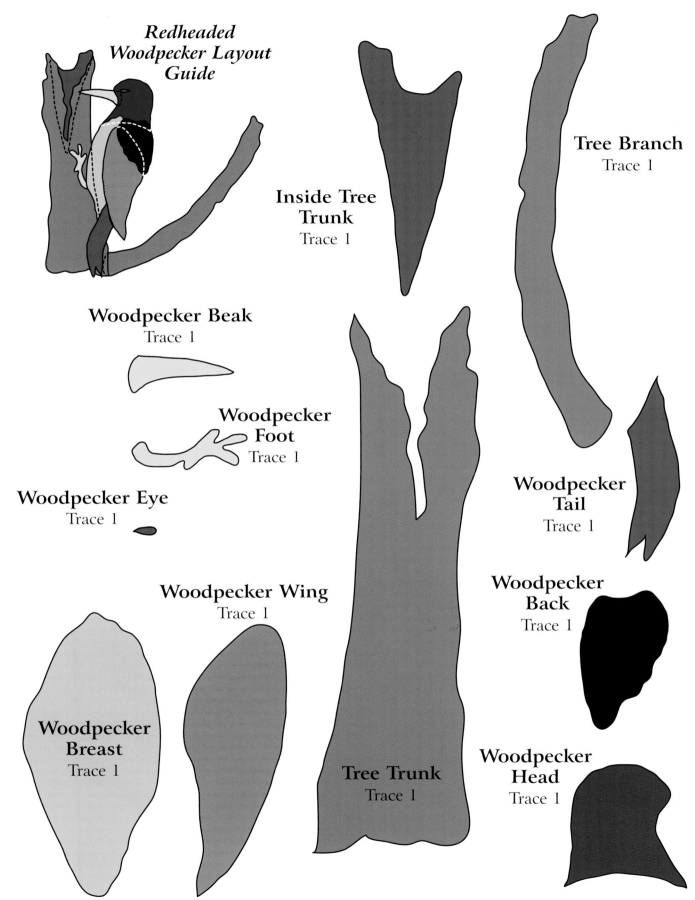

Redheaded Woodpecker Layout Guide

Inside Tree Trunk
Trace 1

Tree Branch
Trace 1

Woodpecker Beak
Trace 1

Woodpecker Foot
Trace 1

Woodpecker Eye
Trace 1

Woodpecker Tail
Trace 1

Woodpecker Wing
Trace 1

Woodpecker Back
Trace 1

Woodpecker Breast
Trace 1

Tree Trunk
Trace 1

Woodpecker Head
Trace 1

21

Completed Birdwatching Layout Guides

Robin

Cardinal

Chickadee

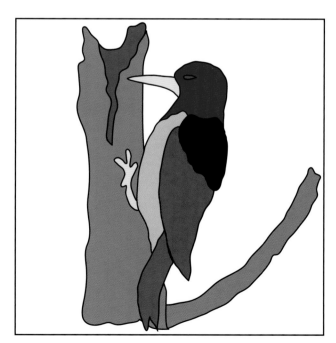

Redheaded Woodpecker

Bird Watching Table Runner

Materials

Refer to the general instructions on pages 10-13 before starting this project.

2/3 yard of yellow marblecake fabric for basket background

3/8 yard of brown check fabric for basket base

1/8 yard of brown woodgrain fabric for basket triangles

1/6 yard of green check fabric for cornerstones

5/8 yard of orange leaves fabric for sashings and binding

7" x 12" piece of variegated green woodgrain fabric for bittersweet stem

4" x 9" piece of olive green woodgrain fabric for green leaves

7" x 9" piece of mustard yellow fabric for full bittersweet buds

6" x 6" square of orange marblecake fabric for half bittersweet buds

3-1/2" x 6-1/2" piece of orange marblecake fabric for center circles

3-1/2" x 3-1/2" square of gold marblecake fabric for center circles

1-1/8 yards of backing fabric

35" x 35" piece of batting

Lightweight paper-backed fusible web

Lightweight tear-away stabilizer

Sulky® threads to match appliqués

Note: Fabrics are based on 44"-wide fabrics that have not been washed. Please purchase accordingly if using prewashed or directional fabrics.

instructions

Cutting

From yellow marblecake fabric:

Cut 1 strip — 6-7/8" x 44";
   from strip cut 2 — 6-7/8" x 6-7/8" squares.
   Cut squares in half diagonally once to make
   4 — 6-7/8" half-square triangles.

Cut 1 strip — 2-7/8" x 44";
   from strip cut 14 — 2-7/8" x 2-7/8" squares.
   Cut squares in half diagonally once to make
   28 — 2-7/8" half-square triangles.

Cut 2 strips — 2-1/2" x 44";
   from strips cut 8 — 2-1/2" x 6-1/2" rectangles.

Cut 1 strip — 4-7/8" x 44";
   from strip cut 2 — 4-7/8" x 4-7/8" squares.
   Cut squares in half diagonally once to make
   4 — 4-7/8" half-square triangles.

From brown check fabric:

Cut 1 strip — 6-7/8" x 44";
   from strip cut 2 — 6-7/8" x 6-7/8" squares.
   Cut squares in half diagonally once to make
   4 — 6-7/8" half-square triangles.

Cut 1 strip — 2-7/8" x 44";
   from strip cut 4 — 2-7/8" x 2-7/8" squares.
   Cut squares in half diagonally once to make
   8 — 2-7/8" half-square triangles.

From brown woodgrain fabric:

Cut 1 strip — 2-7/8" x 44";
   from strip cut 14 — 2-7/8" x 2-7/8" squares.
   Cut squares in half diagonally once to make
   28 — 2-7/8" half-square triangles.

From green check fabric:

Cut 1 strip — 3" x 44";
   from strip cut 9 — 3" x 3" squares.

From orange leaves fabric:

Cut 3 strips — 3" x 44";
   from strip cut 12 — 3" x 10-1/2" rectangles.

Cut 3 strips — 2-3/4" x 44".

Block Assembly

1. Sew together a yellow marblecake 2-7/8" half-square triangle and a brown woodgrain 2-7/8" half-square triangle, as shown. Press the seam allowances toward the dark triangle. Repeat to make 28 Unit A.

Make 28 Unit A

2. Sew 3 Unit A together, as shown. Press seam allowances open. Repeat to make 4 Unit B.

Make 4 Unit B

3. Sew 4 Unit A together, as shown. Press seam allowances open. Repeat to make 4 Unit C.

Make 4 Unit C

4. Sew together a yellow marblecake 6-7/8" half-square triangle and a brown check 6-7/8" half-square triangle, as shown. Press seam allowances toward the dark triangle. Repeat to make 4 Unit D.

Make 4 Unit D

5. Sew a brown check 2-7/8" half-square triangle to a yellow marblecake 2-1/2" x 6-1/2" rectangle, as shown. Press seam allowances toward the dark fabric. Repeat to make 4 Unit E.

Make 4 Unit E

6. Sew a brown check 2-7/8" half-square triangle to a yellow marblecake 2-1/2" x 6-1/2" rectangle, as shown. Press seam allowances toward the dark fabric. Repeat to make 4 Unit F.

Make 4 Unit F

7. Sew a Unit B to a Unit D, as shown. Press the seam allowances open. Repeat to make 4 Unit G.

Make 4 Unit G

8. Sew a Unit C to a Unit G, as shown. Press the seam allowances open. Repeat to make 4 Unit H.

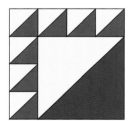

Make 4 Unit H

9. Sew a Unit E to a Unit H, as shown. Press the seam allowances open. Repeat to make 4 Unit I.

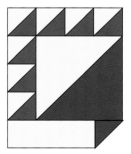

Make 4 Unit I

10. Sew a Unit F to a Unit I, as shown. Press the seam allowances open. Repeat to make 4 Unit J.

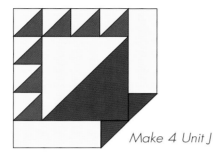

Make 4 Unit J

11. Sew a yellow marblecake 4-7/8" half-square triangle to a Unit J. Press seam allowances open. Repeat to make 4 Basket blocks.

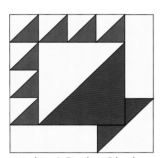

Make 4 Basket Blocks

Table Topper Top Assembly

1. Sew together 3 green check 3" squares and 2 orange leaves 3" x 10-1/2" rectangles, as shown. Press seam allowances toward the sashing. Repeat to make 3 sashing/cornerstone rows.

Make 3 Sashing/Cornerstone Rows

2. Sew together 2 Basket blocks and 3 orange leaves 3" x 10-1/2" rectangles, as shown. Press seam allowances toward the sashing strips. Repeat to make 2 Basket block rows.

Make 2 Basket Block Rows

3. Sew together the sashing/cornerstone rows and the Basket block rows, as shown. Press seam allowances open.

Adding the Appliqués

Note: For each basket, you will need 9 full mustard yellow bittersweet buds showing orange centers and 5 half orange bittersweet buds showing gold centers.

1. Using the appliqué templates on page 28, trace the shapes onto the paper side of the fusible web and cut out as directed.

2. Referring to the Basic Appliqué instructions on pages 10-11, prepare the fabric appliqué pieces. Referring to the layout guide on page 28, position the appliqués and fuse them in place.

3. Use a small zigzag stitch and matching thread around each shape to appliqué it to the topper top. Remember to use tear-away stabilizer when stitching appliqués.

Helpful Hint for Appliquéd Bittersweet Buds — Stitch around the outside of buds first then around the center circle. This will cover up where the stitching ends.

Finishing the Topper

Layer the backing fabric, batting and topper top. Baste the layers together. Hand or machine quilt as desired. Finish the topper by sewing binding to the edges, following the steps in Basic Binding on page 12.

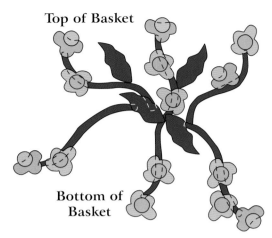

Top of Basket

Bottom of Basket

***Bittersweet Baskets
Layout Guide***

Bottom Right Side of Basket Stem
Trace 4 of each

**Full Bittersweet
Gold Buds**
Trace 36

**Top Right Side
of Basket Stem**
Trace 4 of each

**Center Bottom
of Basket Stem**
Trace 4 of each

**Half Bittersweet
Orange Buds**
Trace 20

**Center Top of
Basket Stem**
Trace 4 of each

**Center Circles
Orange -** Trace 36
Gold - Trace 20

**Top Left Side of
Basket Stem**
Trace 4 of each

Leaf
Trace 16

**Bottom Left Side
of Basket Stem**
Trace 4 of each

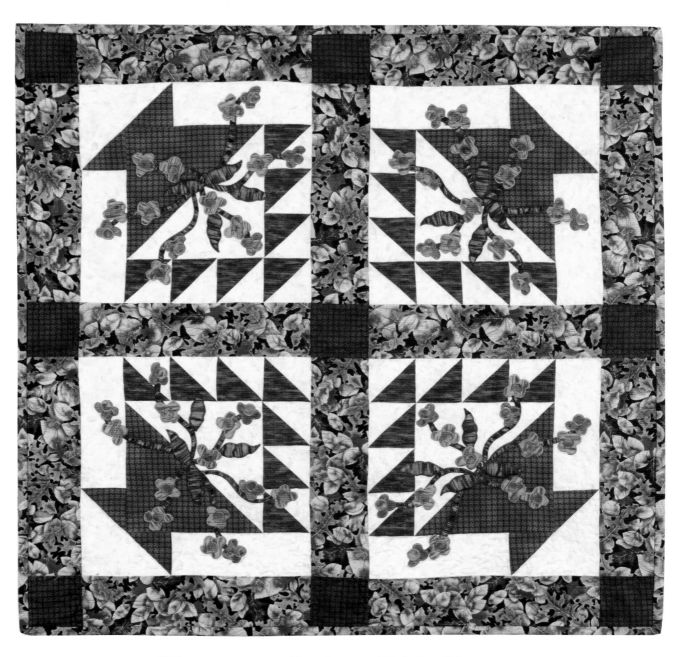

Bittersweet Baskets Table Topper

oval table mat
flying high

Materials

Refer to the general instructions on pages 10-13 before starting this project.

1/2 yard of black marblecake flannel for background and backing

Wool or Flannel

12" x 15" piece of olive green fabric for oval background

7" x 7" square of orange fabric for moon

6" x 6" square of yellow fabric for moon

7" x 8" piece of black fabric for witch

6" x 6" square of black fabric for stars

3" x 8" piece of yellow fabric for stars

Lightweight paper-backed fusible web

Freezer paper

Valdani® Perle Cotton size 12 thread - #506 and #511

DMC® Perle Cotton size 8 thread - #310 and #676

Note: Wool fabrics have been prewashed. Other fabrics used are based on 44"-wide fabrics that have not been washed. Please purchase accordingly if using prewashed or directional fabrics.

instructions

Template Instructions

1. Fold a 12" x 18" sheet of paper in half widthwise. The piece should measure 12" x 9".

2. Trace the inside oval template on page 35 onto paper. Label the fold, tracing and cutting lines. Cut out on cutting line.

3. Lay the template on top of the folded paper from step 1 and cut out on cutting line. Open paper to create the half oval template.

4. Take a piece of freezer paper approximately 19" long and fold in half. Lay the half oval paper template onto freezer paper matching the fold and raw edge at bottom. Trace half oval template onto freezer paper. Cut out on dashed lines (which is 1/4" beyond the traced line).

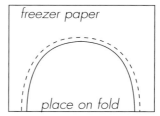

5. Unfold freezer paper for a full oval template. Place shiny side of freezer paper oval on wrong side of olive green wool. Iron. Freezer paper will adhere to wool. Cut out on traced line.

6. Trace oval freezer paper template on fusible web and cut out the center, leaving a 1/2" on inside of oval traced line. Fuse the oval fusible web to the wrong side of the of the olive green wool. Do not remove the 1/2" paper from the fusible web.

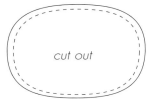

Adding the Appliqués

1. Using the appliqué templates on page 34, trace the shapes onto the paper side of the fusible web and cut out as directed.

2. Referring to the Basic Appliqué instructions on pages 10-11, prepare the fabric appliqué pieces. Referring to the layout guides on page 34, position the appliqués and fuse them in place.

3. Hand appliqué the shapes using a blanket stitch and the following thread colors:

• Large Stars and Witch - #511

• Inner Moon and Small Stars - #676

• Outer Moon - #506

Finishing the Table Mat

1. Fold a 24" x 17" sheet of paper in half widthwise. The piece should measure 12" x 17".

2. Trace the scalloped template on page 35 onto paper. Label the fold, tracing and cutting lines. Cut out on cutting line. Lay the template on top of folded paper from step 1 and cut out on cutting line. Open paper for the half scallop template.

3. Take a piece of freezer paper 24" long and fold in half. The piece should measure 12" x 18". Lay the half scallop paper template onto freezer paper matching the fold and raw edge at bottom. Trace the half scallop template onto freezer paper. Cut out on the dashed lines.

4. Unfold freezer paper for a full scallop template. Place shiny side of freezer paper scallop on wrong side of black flannel marblecake. Iron. Freezer paper will adhere to the flannel. Cut out on traced line.

5. Center the oval appliquéd olive green wool mat on the right side of scalloped black flannel marblecake. Fuse the pieces together. Blanket stitch the oval to scalloped black flannel with black perle cotton.

6. Cut backing piece slightly larger than the appliquéd top. Cut a piece of lightweight fusible web the size of the backing. Lay the fusible web, film side down, on the wrong side of the backing. Fuse the fusible web to backing. When cool, peel the paper off fusible web. Reserve the peeled paper.

7. Lay the wrong side of the appliquéd top on the wrong side of backing. Lay the reserved paper on the mat top and fuse the pieces together.

8. Trim away excess backing with sharp scissors.

9. Blanket stitch around the outside edge with DMC® #310.

Flying High Oval Table Mat

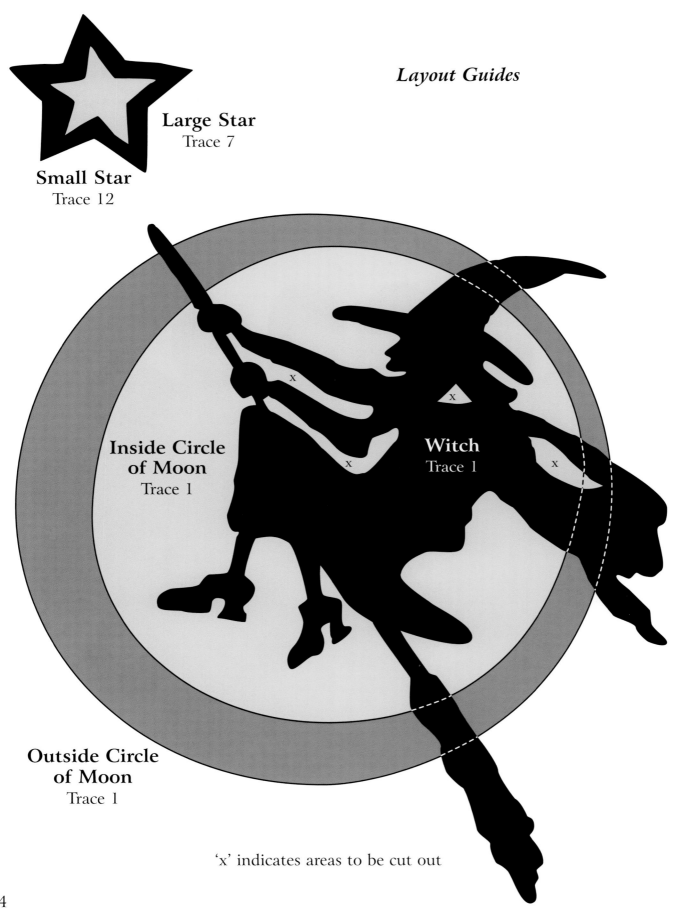

Layout Guides

Large Star
Trace 7

Small Star
Trace 12

**Inside Circle
of Moon**
Trace 1

Witch
Trace 1

**Outside Circle
of Moon**
Trace 1

'x' indicates areas to be cut out

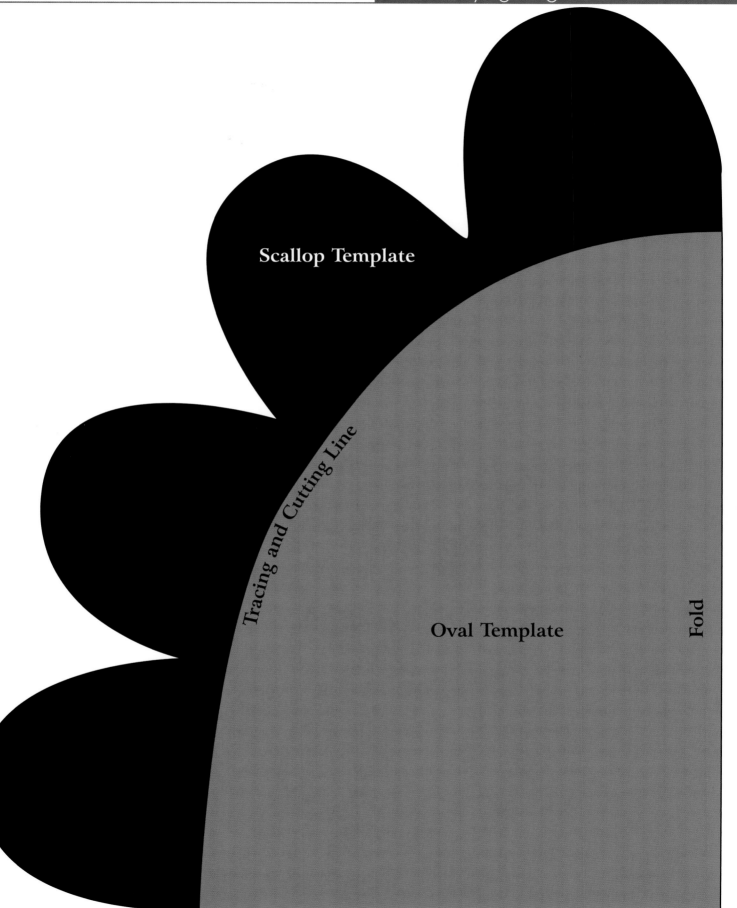

Scallop Template

Tracing and Cutting Line

Oval Template

Fold

table runner *black cat in the pumpkin patch*

Finished size is approximately 14" x 44"

Materials

Refer to the general instructions on pages 10-13 before starting this project.

3/8 yard of ecru twig fabric for block background

1/2 yard of black marblecake fabric for border and binding

1/4 yard of pumpkin marblecake fabric for border

3-1/2" x 3-1/2" square of brown woodgrain fabric for pumpkin stems

6" x 13" piece of medium orange marblecake fabric for pumpkins

8" x 9" piece of olive green woodgrain fabric for small and large leaves

12" x 12" square of black marblecake fabric for cat body parts, head and eyes

4-1/2" x 3-1/2" piece of yellow marblecake fabric for large stars

2" x 3" piece of black marblecake fabric for small inner stars

12-1/2" x 18-1/2" piece of lime green marblecake fabric for cat's body parts outline, head and eyes

3" x 3" square of orange marblecake fabric for parts on cat's face and claws

1" x 1" square of white marblecake fabric for cat's teeth

1-1/4" x 1-1/4" piece of gray marblecake for cat's cheeks

1-1/2 yards of backing fabric

20" x 50" piece of batting

Lightweight paper-backed fusible web

Lightweight tear-away stabilizer

Sulky® threads to match appliqués

Note: Fabrics are based on 44"-wide fabrics that have not been washed. Please purchase accordingly if using prewashed or directional fabrics.

instructions

Cutting

From ecru twig fabric:
   Cut 1 strip — 10-1/2" x 44";
      from strip cut 3 — 10-1/2" x 12-1/2" rectangles.

From black marblecake fabric:
   Cut 2 strips — 2-1/2" x 44";
      from strip cut 32 — 2-1/2" x 2-1/2" squares.
   Cut 3 strips — 2-3/4" x 44".

From pumpkin marblecake fabric:
   Cut 2 strips — 2-1/2" x 44";
      from strip cut 32 — 2-1/2" x 2-1/2" squares.

Table Runner Assembly

1. Sew together 3 pumpkin marblecake 2-1/2" squares and 2 black marblecake 2-1/2" squares, as shown. Press seam allowances toward the dark fabric. Repeat to make 2 Unit A.

Make 2 Unit A

2. Sew together 3 black marblecake 2-1/2" squares and 3 pumpkin marblecake 2-1/2" squares, as shown. Press seam allowances toward the dark fabric. Repeat to make 2 Unit B.

Make 2 Unit B

3. Sew together 11 black marblecake 2-1/2" squares and 11 pumpkin marblecake 2-1/2" squares, as shown. Press the seam allowances toward the dark fabric. Repeat to make 2 Unit C.

Make 2 Unit C

4. Sew together the 2 Unit A, 2 Unit B and 3 ecru twig 10-1/2" x 12-1/2" rectangles, as shown. Press the seam allowances toward the dark fabric.

5. Sew a Unit C to the top and bottom of the runner top, as shown. Press the seam allowances toward the dark fabric.

Adding the Appliqués

1. Using the appliqué templates on pages 38-42, trace the shapes onto the paper side of the fusible web and cut out as directed.

2. Referring to the Basic Appliqué instructions on pages 10-11, prepare the fabric appliqué pieces. Referring to the layout guides on page 43, position the appliqués and fuse them in place.

3. Use a small zigzag stitch and matching thread around each shape to appliqué it to the runner top. Remember to use tear-away stabilizer when stitching appliqués.

Finishing the Runner

Layer the backing fabric, batting and runner top. Baste the layers together. Hand or machine quilt as desired. Finish the runner by sewing binding to the edges, following the steps in Basic Binding on page 12.

Small Star
Trace 8

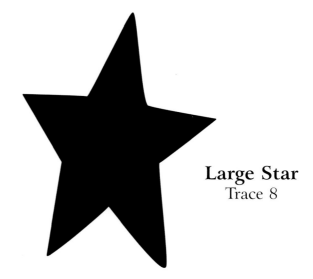

Large Star
Trace 8

Inner Ear
Trace 1 of each

Head
Trace 1

Outer Eyes
Trace 1 of each

Nose
Trace 1 of each

Body
Trace 1

Inner Eyes
Trace 1 of each

Teeth
Trace 1 of each

Center of Eyes
Trace 1 of each

Mouth
Trace 1

Back Claws
Trace 1 of each

Front Claws
Trace 1 of each

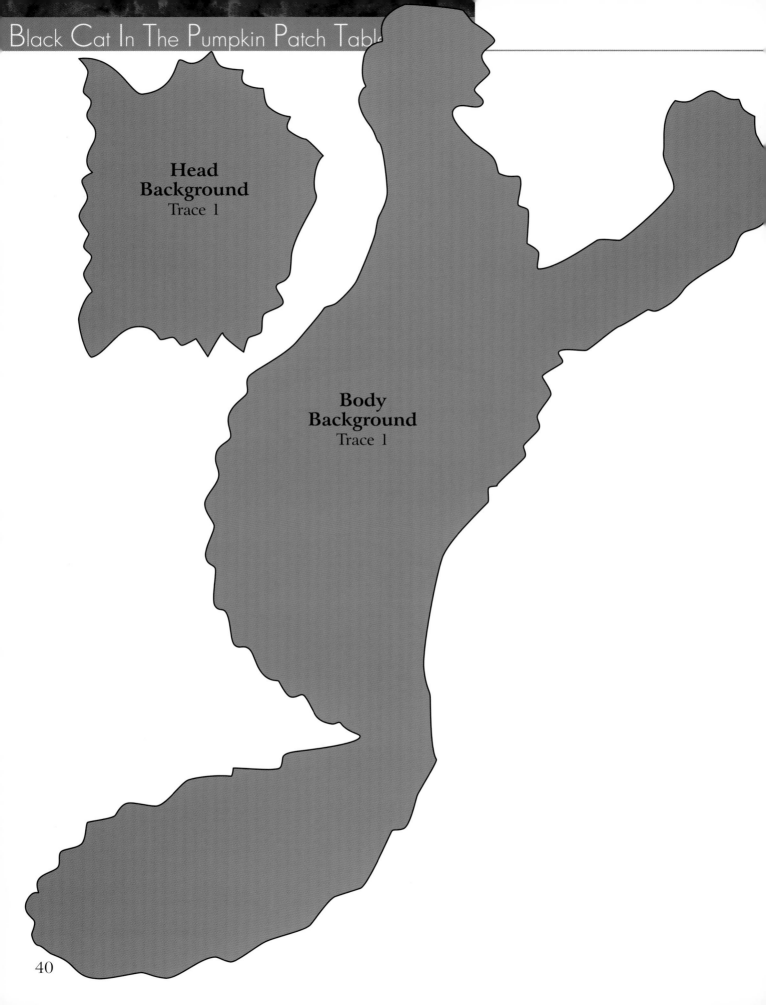

Head Background Trace 1

Body Background Trace 1

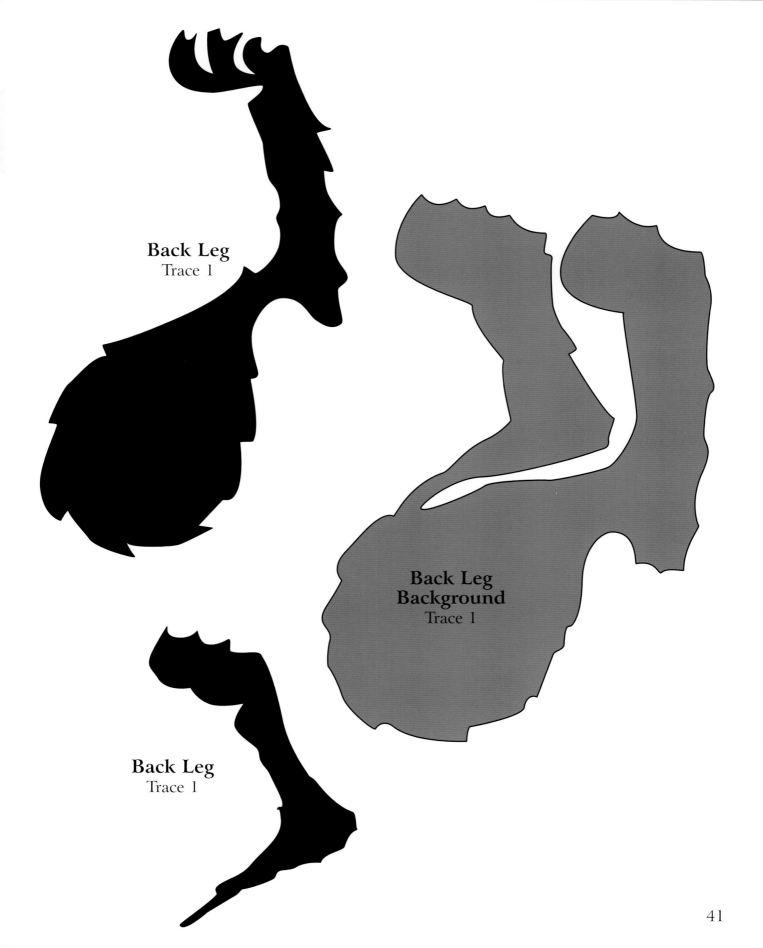

Back Leg
Trace 1

**Back Leg
Background**
Trace 1

Back Leg
Trace 1

Large Leaf
Trace 1 and
1 Reversed

Small Leaf
Trace 1 and
1 Reversed

*Note: Lines inside
pumpkin and leaves
indicate stitching lines
for embellishment.*

Pumpkin Stem
Trace 1 and
1 Reversed

Pumpkin
Trace 1 and
1 Reversed

Cat Layout Guide

Pumpkins & Stars
Layout Guide

Black Cat in the Pumpkin Patch Table Runner

candle mat
black cat

Finished size is approximately 15" x 17"

Materials

Refer to the general instructions on pages 10 -13 before starting this project.

5/8 yard of black marblecake fabric
for background, border and binding

1/8 yard of salmon marblecake fabric for border

12" x 12" square of black marblecake fabric
for cat body parts, head and eyes

3" x 5" piece of yellow marblecake fabric for large stars

2" x 3-1/2" piece of black
marblecake fabric for small inner stars

12-1/2" x 18-1/2" piece of lime green marblecake fabric
for cat's body parts outline, head and eyes

3" x 3" square of orange marblecake fabric for parts on
cat's face and claws

1" x 1" square of white marblecake fabric for cat's teeth

1-1/4" x 1-1/4" square of gray marblecake
for cat's cheeks

5/8 yard of backing fabric

21" x 23" piece of batting

Lightweight paper-backed fusible web

Lightweight tear-away stabilizer

Sulky® threads to match appliqué fabric

*Note: Fabrics are based on 44"-wide fabrics
that have not been washed. Please purchase
accordingly if using prewashed or directional fabrics.*

44

Instructions

Cutting

From black marblecake fabric:
    Cut 1 strip — 10-1/2" x 44";
        from strip cut 1 — 10-1/2" x 12-1/2" rectangle.
    Cut 1 strip — 2-1/2" x 44";
        from strip cut 13 — 2-1/2" x 2-1/2" squares.
    Cut 2 strips — 2-1/2" x 44".

From salmon marblecake fabric:
    Cut 1 strip — 2-1/2" x 44";
        from strip cut 13 — 2-1/2" x 2-1/2" squares.

Candle Mat Assembly

1. Sew together 3 salmon marblecake 2-1/2" squares and 2 black marblecake 2-1/2" squares, as shown. Press the seam allowances toward the dark fabric. Make 1 Unit A.

Make 1 Unit A

2. Sew together 3 black marblecake 2-1/2" squares and 2 salmon marblecake 2-1/2" squares, as shown. Press the seam allowances toward the dark fabric. Make 1 Unit B.

Make 1 Unit B

3. Sew together 4 black marblecake 2-1/2" squares and 4 salmon marblecake 2-1/2" squares, as shown. Press the seam allowances toward the dark fabric. Make 2 Unit C.

Make 2 Unit C

4. Sew Unit A and Unit B to each side of the black marblecake 10-1/2" x 12-1/2" rectangle, as shown. Press seam allowances toward the dark fabric. Make 1 Unit D.

Make 1 Unit D

5. Sew a Unit C to the top and bottom of Unit D, as shown. Press seam allowances toward the dark fabric.

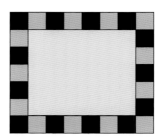

Adding the Appliqués

1. Using the appliqué templates on pages 38-41, trace the shapes onto the paper side of the fusible web and cut out as directed.

2. Referring to the Basic Appliqué instructions on pages 10-11, prepare the fabric appliqué pieces. Referring to the cat layout guide on page 43, position the appliqués and fuse them in place.

3. Use a small zigzag stitch and matching thread around each shape to appliqué it to the candle mat top. Remember to use tear-away stabilizer when stitching appliqués.

Finishing the Mat

Layer the backing fabric, batting and mat top. Baste the layers together. Hand or machine quilt as desired. Finish the mat by sewing binding to the edges, following the steps in Basic Binding on page 12.

table topper
give thanks

Refer to the general instructions on pages 10-13 before starting this project.

3/8 yard of ecru woodgrain fabric for background

1/6 yard of green woodgrain fabric for border cornerstone

1/8 yard of brown woodgrain fabric for pieced border

1/8 yard of red leave fabric for pieced border

1/8 yard of green check fabric for pieced border

1/8 yard of turkey/birch trees fabric for pieced border

3/8 yard of red marbled fabric for pieced border and binding

3-1/2" x 6" piece of turkey feathers fabric for turkey body—part A

3-1/2" x 4" piece of brown woodgrain fabric for turkey body—part B

6-1/2" x 3-1/2" piece of turkey feathers fabric for turkey body—part C

1" x 2-1/4" piece of dark red marbled fabric for waddle

4" x 7" piece of green woodgrain fabric for leaves and stems

6" x 8-1/2" piece of red marbled fabric for words

3-1/2" x 8" piece of orange marblecake fabric for pumpkins

1-1/2" x 3" piece of red marbled fabric for head

2-1/4" x 2-1/2" piece of brown fabric for feet

scrap of black fabric for eye

1" x 1/2" piece of gold fabric for beak

7/8 yard of backing fabric

25" x 31" piece of batting

Lightweight paper-backed fusible web

Lightweight tear-away stabilizer

Sulky® threads to match appliqué fabric

Note: Fabrics are based on 44"-wide fabrics that have not been washed. Please purchase accordingly if using prewashed or directional fabrics.

Instructions

Cutting

From ecru woodgrain fabric:
Cut 1 strip — 11-3/4" x 44";
from strip cut 1 — 11-3/4" x 18" rectangle.

From green woodgrain fabric:
Cut 1 strip — 3-1/2" x 44";
from strip cut 4 — 3-1/2" x 3-1/2" squares.

From brown woodgrain fabric:
Cut 1 strip — 1-3/4" x 44";
from strip cut 8 — 1-3/4" x 3-1/2" rectangles.

From red leaves fabric:
Cut 1 strip — 1-3/4" x 44";
from strip cut 10 — 1-3/4" x 3-1/2" rectangles.

From green check fabric:
Cut 1 strip — 1-3/4" x 44";
from strip cut 10 — 1-3/4" x 3-1/2" rectangles.

From turkey/birch trees fabric:
Cut 1 strip — 1-3/4" x 44";
from strip cut 10 — 1-3/4" x 3-1/2" rectangles.

From red marbled fabric:
Cut 1 strip — 1-3/4" x 44";
from strip cut 8 — 1-3/4" x 3-1/2" rectangles.
Cut 3 strips — 2-3/4" x 44".

Table Topper Assembly

1. Sew together 3 brown woodgrain 1-3/4" x 3-1/2" rectangles, 3 red leaves 1-3/4" x 3-1/2" rectangles, 3 green check 1-3/4" x 3-1/2" rectangles, 3 turkey/birch trees 1-3/4" x 3-1/2" rectangles and 2 red marbled 1-3/4" x 3-1/2" rectangles, as shown. Press all seam allowances toward the right. Repeat to make 2 Unit A.

Make 2 Unit A

2. Sew together 2 red marbled 1-3/4" x 3-1/2" rectangles, 2 turkey/birch trees 1-3/4" x 3-1/2" rectangles, 2 green check 1-3/4" x 3-1/2" rectangles, 2 red leaves 1-3/4" x 3-1/2" rectangles and 1 brown woodgrain 1-3/4" x 3-1/2" rectangle, as shown. Press all seam allowances toward the right. Repeat to make 2 Unit B.

Make 2 Unit B

3. Sew a Unit A to the top and bottom of the ecru woodgrain 11-3/4" x 18" rectangle, as shown. Press seam allowances toward the dark fabric. Make 1 Unit C.

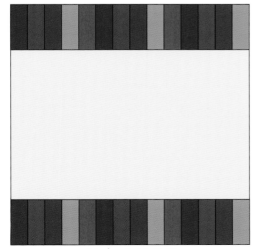

Make 1 Unit C

4. Sew a green woodgrain 3-1/2" x 3-1/2" square on each end of a Unit B, as shown. Press seam allowances toward the dark fabric. Repeat to make 2 Unit D.

Make 2 Unit D

5. Sew a Unit D to each side of Unit C. Press seam allowances toward the dark fabric.

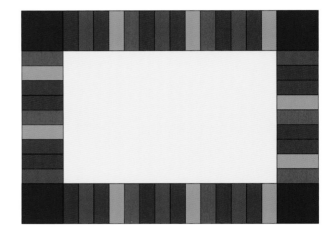

Adding the Appliqués

1. Using the appliqué templates on pages 49-50, trace the shapes onto the paper side of the fusible web and cut out as directed.

2. Referring to the Basic Appliqué instructions on pages 10-11, prepare the fabric appliqué pieces. Referring to the layout guides on pages 49-50, position the appliqués and fuse them in place.

3. Use a small zigzag stitch and matching thread around each shape to appliqué it to the topper top. Remember to use tear-away stabilizer when stitching appliqués.

Finishing the Table Topper

Layer the backing fabric, batting and table topper top. Baste the layers together. Hand or machine quilt as desired. Finish the table topper by sewing binding to the edges, following the steps in Basic Binding on page 12.

Turkey Head
Trace 1

Turkey Layout Guide

Beak
Trace 1

Waddle
Trace 1

Eye
Trace 1

Feet
Trace 1

**Turkey Body—
Part B**
Trace 1

**Turkey Body—
Part C**
Trace 1

**Turkey Body—
Part A**
Trace 1

49

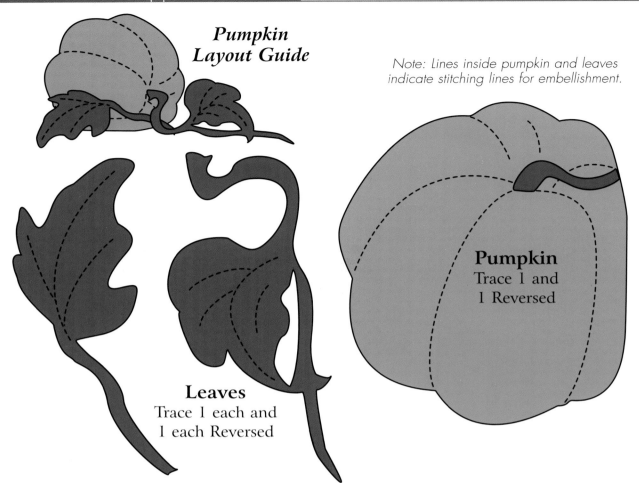

Pumpkin Layout Guide

Note: Lines inside pumpkin and leaves indicate stitching lines for embellishment.

Pumpkin
Trace 1 and
1 Reversed

Leaves
Trace 1 each and
1 each Reversed

Enlarge
letters
120%

GIVE THANKS

Give Thanks Table Topper

table runner
dragonfly summer

Finished size is approximately 20" x 36"

Materials

Refer to the general instructions on pages 10-13 before starting this project.

5/8 yard of pina colada marblecake fabric for center and triangles

1/4 yard of blue velvet pudding marblecake fabric for triangles

1/4 yard of jam session marblecake fabric for triangles

1/4 yard of payaya marblecake fabric for triangles

1/4 yard of cucumber marblecake fabric for triangles

1/4 yard of kiwi marblecake fabric for triangles

1/4 yard of champagne punch marblecake fabric for triangles

1/4 yard of tea leaves marblecake fabric for triangles

1/2 yard of blackberry marblecake fabric for triangles and binding

1/4 yard of limeade marblecake fabric for triangles

11" x 13" piece of bright dark green marblecake fabric for black-eyed susan stems

6" x 7" piece of gold marblecake fabric for black-eyed susan flower part

2" x 2" square of chocolate marblecake for black-eyed susan flower center

7" x 10" piece of light green marblecake fabric for harebell flower stems

5" x 5" square of bright blue marblecake fabric for harebell flowers

1-1/2" x 2-1/2" piece of dark brown woodgrain for small dragonfly body

2-1/2" x 3-1/2" piece of green woodgrain for small dragonfly wings

1-1/2" x 3-1/2" piece of brown woodgrain for large dragonfly body

2-1/2" x 4-1/2" piece of variegated green woodgrain for large dragonfly wings

3/4 yard of backing fabric

26" x 42" piece of batting

Lightweight paper-backed fusible web

Lightweight tear-away stabilizer

Sulky® threads to match appliqués

Note: Fabrics are based on 44"-wide fabrics that have not been washed. Please purchase accordingly if using prewashed or directional fabrics.

Instructions

Cutting

From pina colada marblecake fabric:
   Cut 1 strip — 12-1/2" x 44";
      from strip cut 1 — 12-1/2" x 28-1/2" rectangle.
   Cut 1 strip — 4-7/8" x 44";
      from strip cut 2 — 4-7/8" x 4-7/8" squares.
      Cut squares in half diagonally once to make
      4 — 4-7/8" half-square triangles.

From blue velvet pudding marblecake fabric:
   Cut 1 strip — 4-7/8" x 44";
      from strip cut 3 — 4-7/8" x 4-7/8" squares.
      Cut squares in half diagonally once to make
      6 — 4-7/8" half-square triangles. 1 will not be used.

From jam session marblecake fabric:
   Cut 1 strip — 4-7/8" x 44";
      from strip cut 3 — 4-7/8" x 4-7/8" squares.
      Cut squares in half diagonally once to make
      6 — 4-7/8" half-square triangles. 1 will not be used.

From papaya marblecake fabric:

Cut 1 strip — 4-7/8" x 44";

from strip cut 3 — 4-7/8" x 4-7/8" squares.
Cut squares in half diagonally once to make
6 — 4-7/8" half-square triangles. 1 will not be used.

From cucumber marblecake fabric:

Cut 1 strip — 4-7/8" x 44";

from strip cut 3 — 4-7/8" x 4-7/8" squares.
Cut squares in half diagonally once to make
6 — 4-7/8" half-square triangles. 1 will not be used.

From kiwi marblecake fabric:

Cut 1 strip — 4-7/8" x 44";

from strip cut 3 — 4-7/8" x 4-7/8" squares.
Cut squares in half diagonally once to make
6 — 4-7/8" half-square triangles. 1 will not be used.

From champagne punch marblecake fabric:

Cut 1 strip — 4-7/8" x 44";

from strip cut 3 — 4-7/8" x 4-7/8" squares.
Cut squares in half diagonally once to make
6 — 4-7/8" half-square triangles. 1 will not be used.

From tea leaves marblecake fabric:

Cut 1 strip — 4-7/8" x 44";

from strip cut 3 — 4-7/8" x 4-7/8" squares.
Cut squares in half diagonally once to make
6 — 4-7/8" half-square triangles. 1 will not be used.

From blackberry marblecake fabric:

Cut 1 strip — 4-7/8" x 44";

from strip cut 3 — 4-7/8" x 4-7/8" squares.
Cut squares in half diagonally once to make
6 — 4-7/8" half-square triangles. 1 will not be used.
Cut 3 strips — 2-1/2" x 44".

From limeade marblecake fabric:

Cut 1 strip — 4-7/8" x 44";

from strip cut 2 — 4-7/8" x 4-7/8" squares.
Cut squares in half diagonally once to make
4 — 4-7/8" half-square triangles.

Block Assembly

1. Sew together a blue velvet pudding marblecake 4-7/8" half-square triangle and a jam session marblecake 4-7/8" half-square triangle, as shown. Press seam allowances toward the dark triangle. Repeat to make 5 Unit A.

Make 5 Unit A

2. Repeat step 1 using the following color combinations:

- papaya marblecake and cucumber marblecake half-square triangles. Make 5 Unit B.

- kiwi marblecake and champagne punch marblecake half-square triangles. Make 5 Unit C.

- tea leaves marblecake and blackberry marblecake half-square triangles. Make 5 Unit D.

- pina colada marblecake and limeade marblecake half-square triangles. Make 4 Unit E.

Make 5 Unit B   *Make 5 Unit C*   *Make 5 Unit D*   *Make 4 Unit E*

Border Assembly

1. Sew together a Unit D, a Unit E and a Unit A, as shown. Press seam allowances open. Make 1 Unit A.

Make 1 Unit A

2. Sew together a Unit C, a Unit B and a Unit A, as shown. Press seam allowances open. Make 1 Unit B.

Make 1 Unit B

3. Sew together 2 Unit C, 2 Unit B, 2 Unit A, 1 Unit E and 2 Unit D, as shown. Press seam allowances open. Make 1 Unit C.

Make 1 Unit C

4. Sew together 2 Unit B, 2 Unit C, 2 Unit D, 2 Unit E and 1 Unit A, as shown. Press seam allowances open. Make 1 Unit D.

Make 1 Unit D

Table Runner Assembly

1. Sew Unit A to the left side and Unit B to the right side of the pina colada marblecake 12-1/2" x 28-1/2" rectangle, as shown. Press seam allowances open. Make 1 Unit E.

Make 1 Unit E

2. Sew Unit C to the top and Unit D to the bottom of Unit E, as shown. Press seam allowances open.

Adding the Appliqués

1. Using the appliqué templates on pages 56-58, trace the shapes onto the paper side of the fusible web and cut out as directed.

2. Referring to the Basic Appliqué instructions on pages 10-11, prepare the fabric appliqué pieces. Referring to the layout guides on pages 56-58, position and fuse the appliqués in place.

3. Use a small zigzag stitch and matching thread around each shape to appliqué it to the runner top. Remember to use tear-away stabilizer when stitching appliqués.

Finishing the Runner

Layer the backing fabric, batting and runner top. Baste the layers together. Hand or machine quilt as desired. Finish the runner by sewing binding to the edges, following the steps in Basic Binding on page 12.

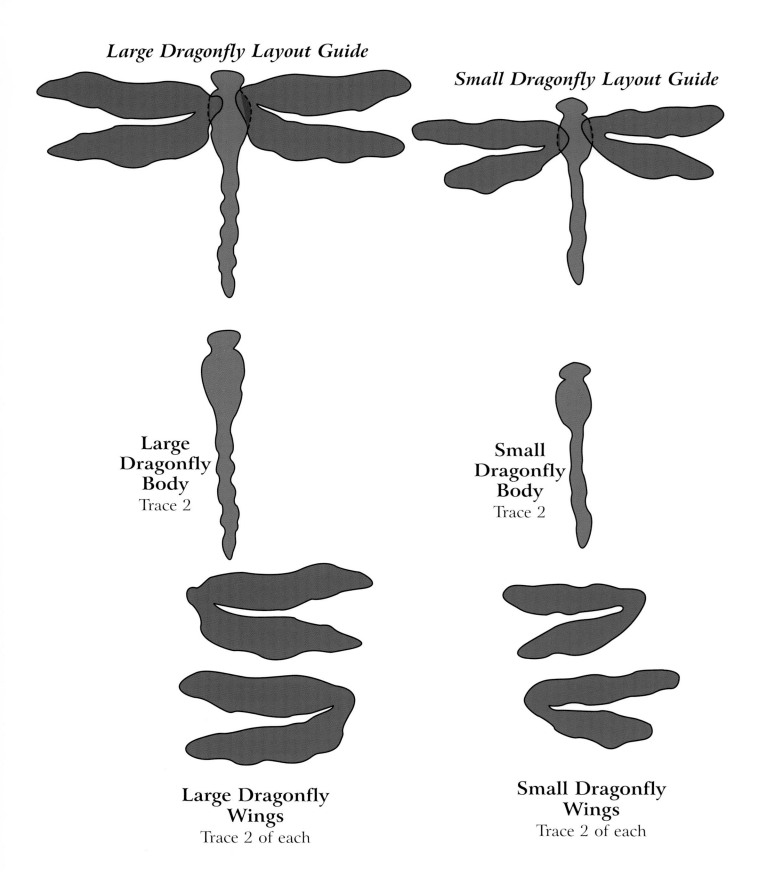

Large Dragonfly Layout Guide

Small Dragonfly Layout Guide

Large Dragonfly Body
Trace 2

Small Dragonfly Body
Trace 2

Large Dragonfly Wings
Trace 2 of each

Small Dragonfly Wings
Trace 2 of each

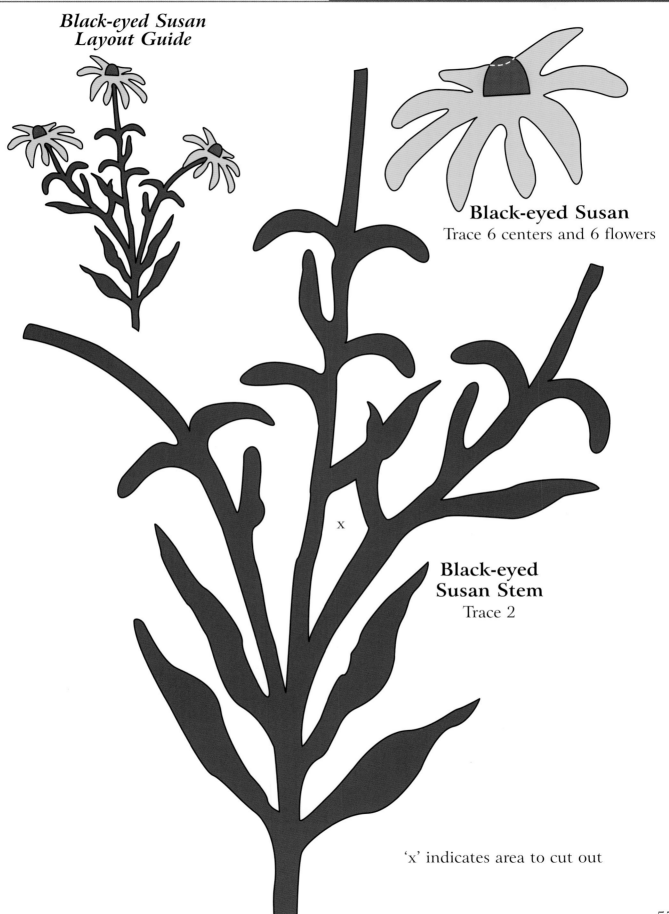

**Black-eyed Susan
Layout Guide**

Black-eyed Susan
Trace 6 centers and 6 flowers

x

**Black-eyed
Susan Stem**
Trace 2

'x' indicates area to cut out

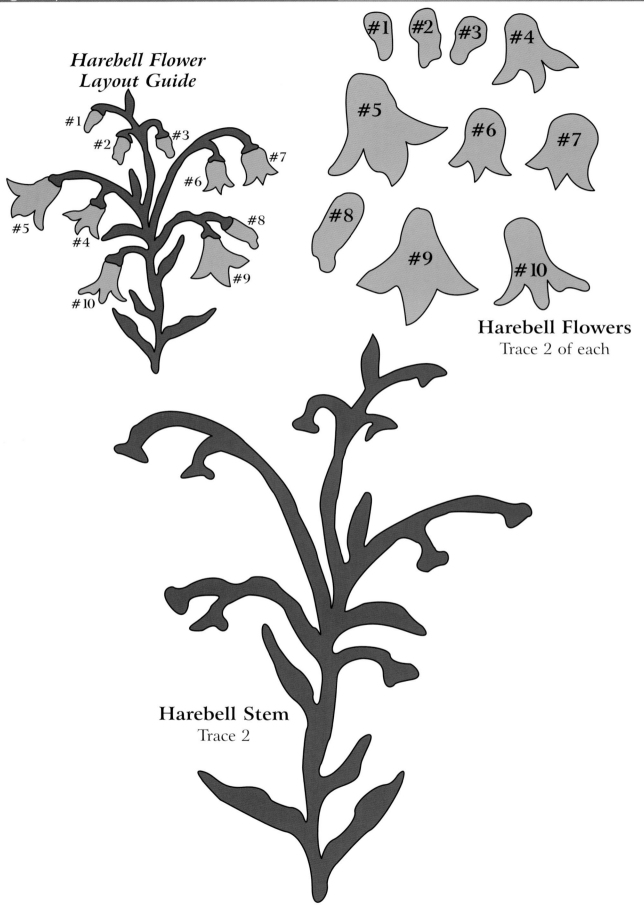

**Harebell Flower
Layout Guide**

#1
#2
#3
#7
#6
#5
#4
#8
#9
#10

#1 #2 #3 #4
#5
#6 #7
#8
#9 #10

Harebell Flowers
Trace 2 of each

Harebell Stem
Trace 2

Dragonfly Summer Table Runner

table runner
holiday poinsettia

Finished size is approximately 19" x 42"

Materials

Refer to the general instructions on pages 10-13 before starting this project.

3/8 yard of ecru woodgrain fabric for center

1/4 yard of brown woodgrain fabric for inner border

7/8 yard of green texture fabric for outer border and binding

4" x 11" piece of dark green woodgrain fabric for leaves

5-1/2" x 14" piece of light red marblecake fabric for poinsettia top layer (top layer of flower)

5-1/2" x 14" piece of dark red marblecake fabric for poinsettia (bottom part of flower)

10" x 14" piece of olive green woodgrain fabric for pine branches

8-1/2" x 8" piece of brown woodgrain fabric for pinecones

1-3/8 yards of backing

25" x 48" piece of batting

Lightweight paper-backed fusible web

Lightweight tear-away stabilizer

Sulky® threads to match appliqués

9 Small Pearl Buttons

Note: Fabrics are based on 44"-wide fabrics that have not been washed. Please purchase accordingly if using prewashed or directional fabrics.

instructions

Cutting

From ecru woodgrain fabric:
  Cut 1 strip — 9-1/2" x 44";
    from strip cut 1 — 9-1/2" x 32-1/2" rectangle.

From brown woodgrain fabric:
  Cut 3 strips — 1-1/2" x 44";
    from strip cut 1 strip into 2 — 1-1/2" x 9-1/2" rectangles.

From green texture fabric:
  Cut 3 strips — 4-1/2" x 44".
  Cut 4 strips — 2-3/4" x 44".

Table Runner Assembly

1. Sew a brown woodgrain 1-1/2" x 9-1/2" rectangle to each end of the ecru woodgrain 9-1/2" x 32-1/2" rectangle, as shown. Press seam allowances toward the dark fabric.

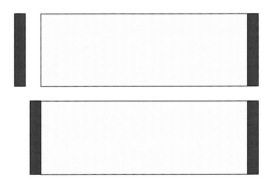

2. Measure the width of the table runner top through the center for the top and bottom border measurement. Use this measurement to cut 2 lengths from the brown woodgrain 1-1/2"-wide strips. Sew the strips to the top and bottom edges of the table runner. Press seam allowances toward the dark fabric.

3. Measure the length of the runner top through the center to determine the side border measurement. Cut 2 strips from the green texture 4-1/2" wide strips to the length needed. Sew to each side of the runner. Press seam allowances toward the dark fabric.

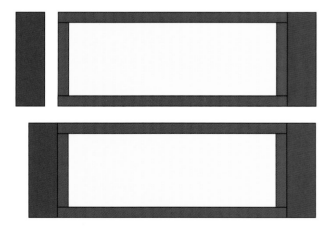

4. Measure the width of the table runner top through the center for the top and bottom border measurement. Use this measurement to cut 2 strips from the green texture 4–1/2"-wide strips. Sew

the strips to the top and bottom edges of the runner. Press seam allowances toward the dark fabric.

Adding the Appliqués

1. Using the appliqué templates on pages 63-64 trace the shapes onto the paper side of the fusible web and cut out as directed.

2. Referring to the Basic Appliqué instructions on pages 10-11, prepare the fabric appliqué pieces. Referring to the layout guide on page 63, position the appliqués and fuse them in place.

3. Use a small zigzag stitch and matching thread around each shape to appliqué it to the table runner top. Remember to use tear-away stabilizer when stitching appliqués.

Finishing the Runner

Layer the backing fabric, batting and runner top. Baste the layers together. Hand or machine quilt as desired. Finish the table runner by sewing binding to the edges, following the steps in Basic Binding on page 12.

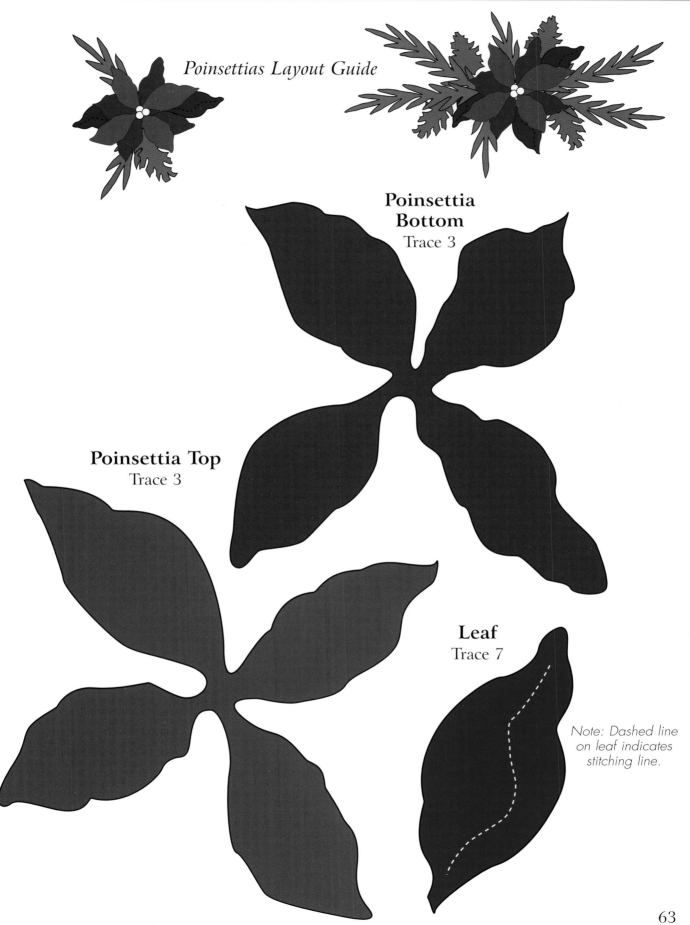

Poinsettias Layout Guide

Poinsettia Bottom
Trace 3

Poinsettia Top
Trace 3

Leaf
Trace 7

Note: Dashed line on leaf indicates stitching line.

Large Pinecone
Trace 1 and 1 Reversed

Long Pine Branch
Trace 4

**Small
Pinecone**
Trace 4

Short Pine Branch
Trace 6

Holiday Poinsettia Table Runner

table runner
nestled in the woods

Finished size is approximately 16" x 48"

Materials

Refer to the general instructions on pages 10-13 before starting this project.

1/2 yard of yellow cloud fabric for large and small triangles

1/3 yard of gold woodgrain fabric for large triangles

1/4 yard of olive/green texture fabric for small triangles

1/4 yard of brown marblecake fabric for inner border

1-1/8 yards of cream background trees fabric for outer border and binding

1/4 yard of gold marblecake fabric for outer border cornerstones

7" x 8" piece of chocolate brown marblecake fabric for deer body

1" x 2-1/2" piece of cream marblecake fabric for deer chest

4-1/2" x 5-1/2" piece of black marblecake fabric for deer body

1" x 1" square of gold marblecake fabric for bear nose

4" x 6" piece of dark brown woodgrain fabric for cabin roof

4-1/2" x 6" piece of medium brown woodgrain fabric for cabin logs and door

1-5/8 yards of backing fabric

24" x 56" piece of batting

Lightweight paper-backed fusible web

Lightweight tear-away stabilizer

Sulky® threads to match appliqué fabric

Note: Fabrics are based on 44"-wide fabrics that have not been washed. Please purchase accordingly if using prewashed or directional fabrics.

instructions

Cutting

From yellow cloud fabric:
 Cut 2 strips — 2-7/8" x 44";
  from strip cut 16 — 2-7/8" x 2-7/8" squares.
  Cut squares in half diagonally once to make
  32 half-square triangles.
 Cut 1 strip — 8-7/8" x 44";
  from strip cut 2 — 8-7/8" x 8-7/8" squares.
  Cut squares in half diagonally once to make
  4 half-square triangles. 1 will not be used.

From gold woodgrain fabric:
 Cut 1 strip — 8-7/8" x 44";
  from strip cut 2 — 8-7/8" x 8-7/8" squares.
  Cut squares in half diagonally once to make
  4 half-square triangles. 1 will not be used.

From olive/green texture fabric:
 Cut 2 strips — 2-7/8" x 44";
  from strip cut 16 — 2-7/8" x 2-7/8" squares.
  Cut squares in half diagonally once to make
  32 half-square triangles.

From brown marblecake fabric:
 Cut 3 strips — 1-1/2" x 44".

From cream background trees fabric:
 Cut 1 strip — 11-1/2" x 44";
  from strip cut 2 — 4-1/2" x 11-1/2" rectangles.
 Cut 3 strips — 4-1/2" x 44".
 Cut 4 strips — 2-1/2" x 44".

From gold marblecake fabric:
 Cut 1 strip — 4-1/2" x 44";
  from strip cut 4 — 4-1/2" x 4-1/2" squares.

Flying Geese Block Assembly

1. Sew together a yellow cloud 2-7/8" half-square triangle and an olive/green texture 2-7/8" half-square triangle, as shown. Press seam allowances toward the dark fabric. Repeat to make 32 Unit A.

Make 32 Unit A

2. Sew 2 Unit A together, as shown. Press the seam allowances open. Repeat to make 16 Unit B.

Make 16 Unit B

3. Sew together 4 Unit B, as shown. Press the seam allowances open. Repeat to make 4 Unit C.

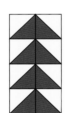

Make 4 Unit C

Triangle Square Assembly

1. Sew together a yellow cloud 8-7/8" half-square triangle and a gold woodgrain 8-7/8" half-square triangle, as shown. Press seam allowances toward the dark fabric. Repeat to make 3 Unit D.

Make 3 Unit D

Runner Assembly

Sew together 4 Unit C and 3 Unit D, as shown. Press seam allowances open.

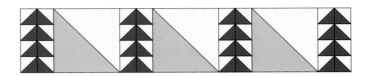

Borders

1. Measure the length of the runner top through the center to determine the side border measurement. Cut 2 strips from the brown marblecake 1-1/2"-wide strips to the length needed. Sew to each side of the runner. Press seam allowances toward the dark fabric.

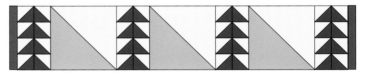

2. Measure the width of the table runner top through the center for the top and bottom border measurement. Use this measurement to cut 2 lengths from the brown marblecake 1-1/2"-wide strips. Sew the strips to the top and bottom edges of the runner. Press seam allowances toward the dark fabric.

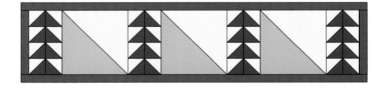

3. Measure the width of the table runner top through the center for the top and bottom border measurement. Use this measurement to cut 2 lengths from the cream background trees 4-1/2"-wide strips.

4. Measure the length of the runner top through the center to determine the side border measurement. Cut 2 strips to the length needed from the cream background trees 4-1/2" x 11-1/2" rectangles.

5. Sew the side border cream background trees 4-1/2"-wide strips to each side of the runner. Press seam allowances toward the dark fabric.

6. Sew the gold marblecake 4-1/2" x 4-1/2" squares to each end of the cream background trees 4-1/2" top and bottom border strips from step 3. Press seam allowances toward the dark fabric.

7. Sew the top and bottom border strips to the runner, as shown. Press seam allowances toward the dark fabric.

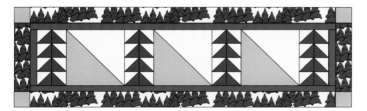

Adding the Appliqués

1. Using the appliqué templates on pages 70-72, trace the shapes onto the paper side of the fusible web and cut out as directed.

2. Referring to the Basic Appliqué instructions on pages 10-11, prepare the fabric appliqué pieces. Referring to the layout guide below, position the appliqués and fuse them in place.

3. Use a small zigzag stitch and matching thread around each shape to appliqué it to the runner top. Remember to use tear-away stabilizer when stitching appliqués.

Finishing the Runner

Layer the backing fabric, batting and runner top. Baste the layers together. Hand or machine quilt as desired. Finish the runner by sewing binding to the edges, following the steps in Basic Binding on page 12.

Nestled In The Woods
Layout Guide

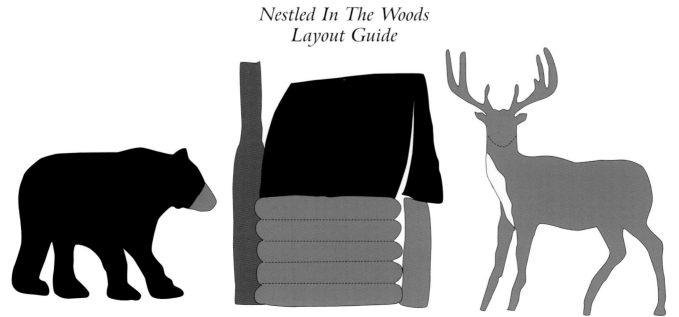

**Log Cabin
Roof Peak**
Trace 1

Chimney
Trace 1

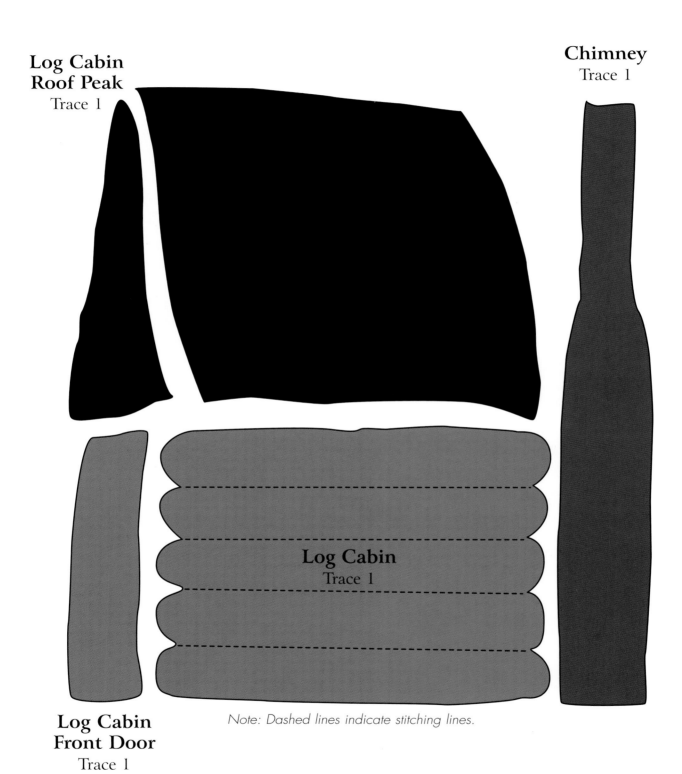

Log Cabin
Trace 1

**Log Cabin
Front Door**
Trace 1

Note: Dashed lines indicate stitching lines.

Deer Body
Trace 1

Deer Chest
Trace 1

Note: Dashed line is embellishment on deer.

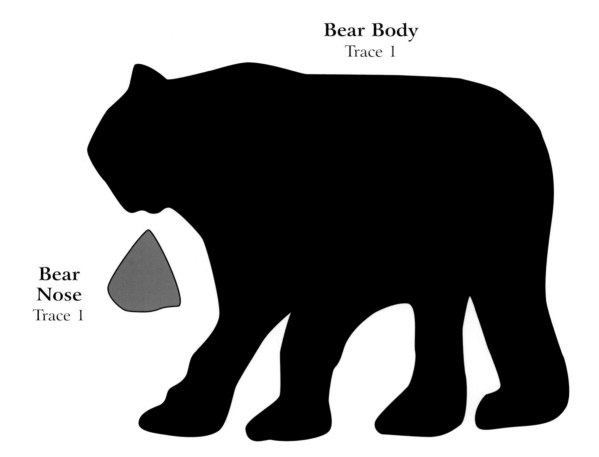

Bear Body
Trace 1

Bear Nose
Trace 1

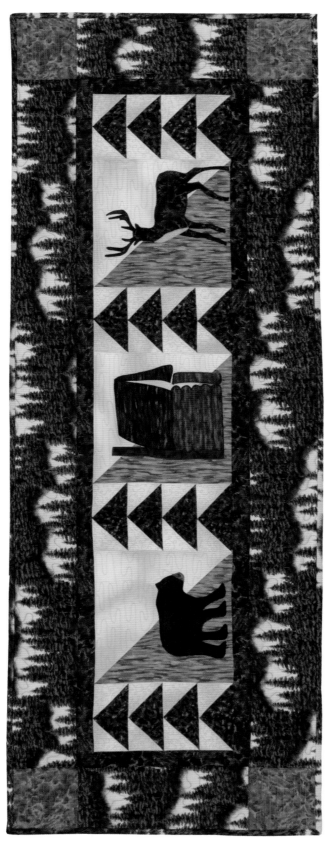

Nestled In The Woods Table Runner

table runner
north woods winter

Finished size is approximately 25" x 39"

Materials

Refer to the general instructions on pages 10-13 before starting this project.

1/2 yard of blue fish marblecake fabric for center

1 yard of berry blue marblecake fabric for inner border, middle border, outer border and binding

1/8 yard of blue velvet pudding marblecake fabric for middle border

1/8 yard of tea leaves marblecake fabric for middle border

1/8 yard of bahama mama blue marblecake fabric for middle border

18" x 22" piece of white marblecake fabric for full and half snowflakes

6" x 8" piece of red marblecake fabric for red part of snowman hat

5-1/2" x 8" piece of tan marblecake fabric for tan part of snowman hat

3" x 4" piece of black marblecake fabric for eyes, eyebrows and smile

2" x 3" piece of orange marblecake fabric for nose

5-1/2" x 4" piece of red marblecake fabric for snowman collar

1-3/8 yards of backing fabric

32" x 46" piece of batting

Lightweight paper-backed fusible web

Lightweight tear-away stabilizer

Sulky® threads to match appliqué fabric

Note: Fabrics are based on 44"-wide fabrics that have not been washed. Please purchase accordingly if using prewashed or directional fabrics.

instructions

Cutting

From blue fish marblecake fabric:
   Cut 1 strip — 12" x 44";
      from strip cut 1 — 12" x 26" rectangle.

From berry blue marblecake fabric:
   Cut 3 strips — 1-1/4" x 44";
      from strips cut 2 — 1-1/4" x 12" rectangles and
      2 — 1-1/4" x 27-1/2" rectangles.
   Cut 5 strips — 3-1/2" x 44";
      from 2 strips cut 20 — 3-1/2" x 3-1/2" squares.
   Cut 4 strips — 2-3/4" x 44".

From blue velvet pudding marblecake fabric:
   Cut 1 strip — 2-1/2" x 44";
      from strip cut 6 — 2-1/2" x 3-1/2" rectangles.

From tea leaves marblecake fabric:
   Cut 1 strip — 2-1/2" x 44";
      from strip cut 5 — 2-1/2" x 3-1/2" rectangles.

From bahama mama blue marblecake fabric:
   Cut 1 strip — 2-1/2" x 44";
      from strip cut 5 — 2-1/2" x 3-1/2" rectangles.

Pieced Border Assembly

1. Sew together 3 berry blue marblecake 3-1/2" x 3-1/2" squares, 1 blue velvet pudding marblecake 2-1/2" x 3-1/2" rectangle and 1 tea leaves marblecake 2-1/2" x 3-1/2" rectangle, as shown. Press seam allowances toward the dark fabric. Make 1 Unit A.

Make 1 Unit A

2. Sew together 3 berry blue marblecake 3-1/2" x 3-1/2" squares, 1 blue velvet pudding marblecake 2-1/2" x 3-1/2" rectangle and 1 bahama mama marblecake 2-1/2" x 3-1/2" rectangle, as shown. Press seam allowances toward the dark fabric. Make 1 Unit B.

Make 1 Unit B

3. Sew together 7 berry blue marblecake 3-1/2" x 3-1/2" squares, 2 blue velvet pudding marblecake 2-1/2" x 3-1/2" rectangles, 2 bahama mama blue marblecake 2-1/2" x 3-1/2" rectangles and 2 tea leaves marblecake 2-1/2" x 3-1/2" rectangles, as shown. Press seam allowances toward the dark fabric. Make 1 Unit C.

Make 1 Unit C

4. Sew together 7 berry blue marblecake 3-1/2" x 3-1/2" squares, 2 bahama mama blue marblecake 2-1/2" x 3-1/2" rectangles, 2 blue velvet pudding marblecake 2-1/2" x 3-1/2" rectangles and 2 tea leaves marblecake 2-1/2" x 3-1/2" rectangles together, as shown. Press seam allowances toward the dark fabric. Make 1 Unit D.

Make 1 Unit D

Runner Assembly

1. Sew a berry blue marblecake 1-1/4" x 12" rectangle to each side of the blue fish marblecake 12" x 26" rectangle. Press seam allowances toward the dark fabric.

2. Sew a berry blue marblecake 1-1/4" x 27-1/2" rectangle to the top and bottom of the runner top. Press seam allowances toward the dark fabric.

3. Sew Unit A to the left side of the runner top, as shown. Press seam allowances toward the dark fabric.

4. Sew Unit B to the right side of the runner top, as shown. Press seam allowances toward the dark fabric.

5. Sew Unit C to the top of the runner top, as shown. Press seam allowances toward the dark fabric.

6. Sew Unit D to the bottom of the runner top, as shown. Press seam allowances toward the dark fabric.

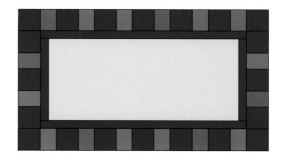

Border Assembly

1. Measure the length of the runner top through the center to determine the side border measurement. Cut 2 strips from the berry blue marblecake 3-1/2"-wide strips to the length needed. Sew to each side of the runner. Press seam allowances toward the dark fabric.

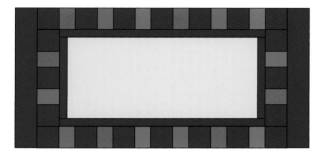

2. Measure the width of the table runner top through the center for the top and bottom border measurement. Use this measurement to cut 2 lengths from the berry blue marblecake 3-1/2"-wide strips. Sew the strips to the top and bottom edges of the table runner. Press seam allowances toward the dark fabric.

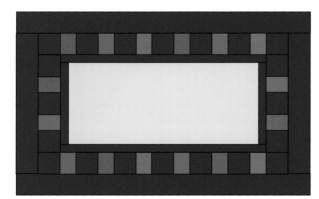

Adding the Appliqués

1. Using the appliqué templates on pages 78-79, trace the shapes onto the paper side of the fusible web and cut out as directed.

2. Referring to the Basic Appliqué instructions on pages 10-11, prepare the fabric appliqué pieces. Referring to the layout guide on page 78, position the appliqués and fuse them in place.

3. Use a small zigzag stitch and matching thread around each shape to appliqué it to the runner top. Remember to use tear-away stabilizer when stitching appliqués.

Finishing the Runner

Layer the backing fabric, batting and runner top. Baste the layers together. Hand or machine quilt as desired. Finish the runner by sewing binding to the edges, following the steps in Basic Binding on page 12.

North Woods Winter Table Runner

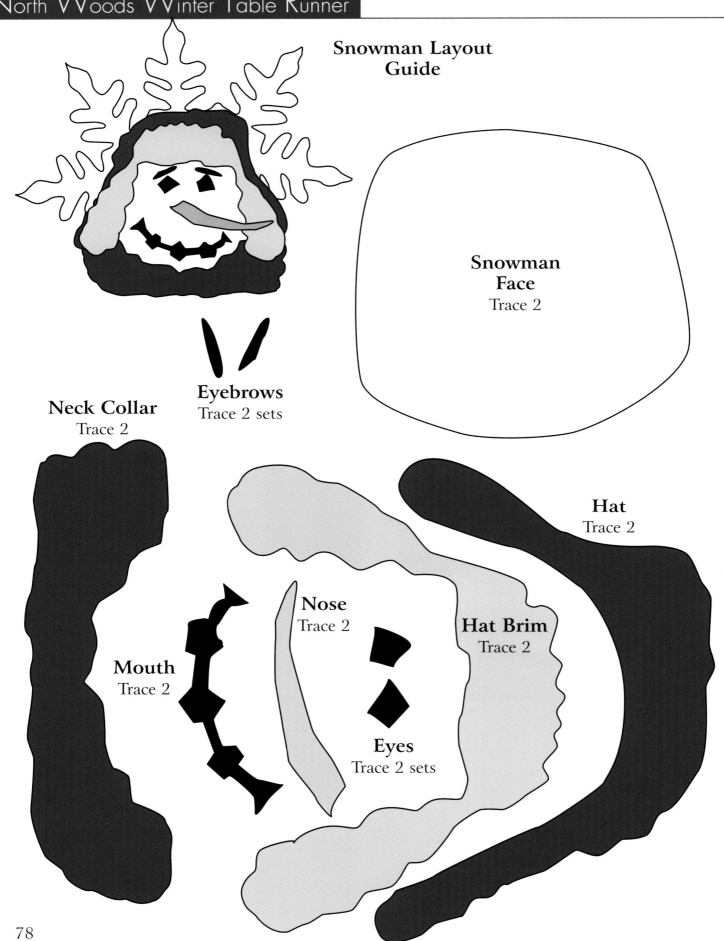

Snowman Layout
Guide

Snowman
Face
Trace 2

Eyebrows
Trace 2 sets

Neck Collar
Trace 2

Hat
Trace 2

Nose
Trace 2

Hat Brim
Trace 2

Mouth
Trace 2

Eyes
Trace 2 sets

78

Enlarge 110%

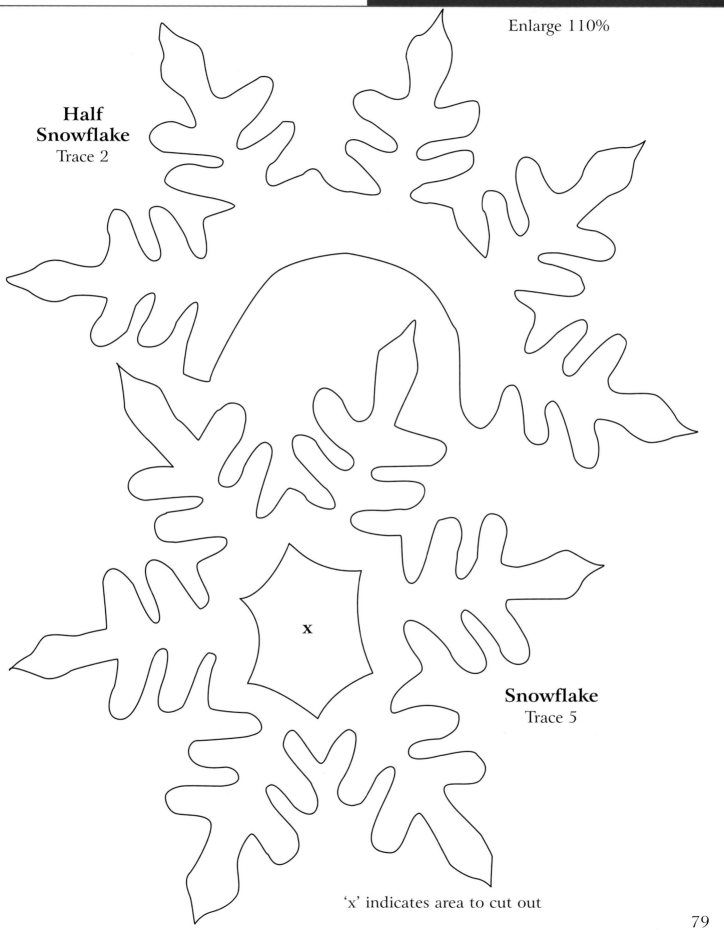

**Half
Snowflake**
Trace 2

Snowflake
Trace 5

x

'x' indicates area to cut out

penny table topper
northern exposure

Materials

Refer to the general instructions on pages 10-13 before starting this project.

Note: Project can be sewn in wool, flannel or cotton. Project shown is made using wool.

25" x 25" square of black wool or black marblecake flannel for background

16" x 18" piece of tan wool for penny circle and small center star

8" x 8" square of red plaid wool for large red background star

9" x 10" piece of green wool for tall tree branches

6-1/2" x 8-1/2" piece of gold wool for tall tree trunks

3" x 3-1/2" piece of brown wool for deer head and body

2" x 5" piece of dark brown wool for skis

1-1/2" x 4" piece of gray wool for ski poles

2-1/2" x 3" piece of brown wool for moose body

1-1/2" x 2" piece of gold wool for moose antlers

3" x 3-1/2" piece of green wool for small tree branches

1" x 4" piece of brown wool for small tree trunks

3-1/2" x 4-1/2" piece of gold wool for snowshoes

1-1/2" x 4" piece of brown wool for snowshoe poles

3-1/4" x 4" piece of black wool for bear body

1" x 1" square of gold wool for bear nose

3" x 3-1/2" piece of light brown wool for pinecones

1" x 5" piece of light green wool for pine branches

2-1/2" x 3-1/2" piece of dark brown wool for log cabin roof

2" x 3-1/2" piece of medium brown wool for cabin logs

26" x 26" square of black marblecake flannel for backing

Lightweight paper-backed fusible web

Freezer paper

Valdani® Perle Cotton size 12 thread - #0178, #78, #M90, #0154, #P12, #0519, #1645, #1 and Gray

Note: Yardage requirements are based on 44" wide unwashed flannel fabric. Please purchase accordingly if using prewashed, directional fabrics or felted wool. The wool fabrics in this project were prewashed.

Instructions

Background Circle Template Instructions

1. Cut 2 strips of freezer paper 18" x 28". On dull side of paper, tape the 2 sheets together. Trim to a 26" x 26" square.

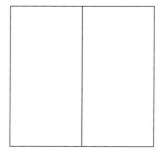

2. Fold the 26" x 26" square in half. It should measure 13" x 26"

3. Fold again to create a double fold. It should measure 13" x 13".

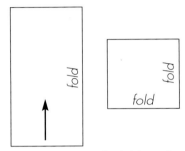

4. Fold again to create a triple fold. It should be cone shaped.

Cutting Circle Template

1. At the bottom of the folded freezer paper point, place a clear acrylic ruler on the 12-1/4" mark. Keeping your fingers pressed down firmly on the 12-1/4" point of the ruler, slowly move the ruler to the right marking dashed lines across the top of folded paper. Remove the ruler and connect the dashes to make one solid line. This is your cutting line for the 24-1/2" circle. Hold all layers of freezer paper tightly and cut on the curved solid line.

2. Open freezer paper to the 24-1/2" circle template. Lay the freezer paper template shiny side down on the wrong side of the wool or cotton fabric background and iron. Cool and cut around the outside edge of the template. Reserve the peeled paper for use in finishing the table topper.

Penny Circles Appliqués Background

Helpful Hint: Trace the circle template onto a piece of cardboard or a plastic template sheet. Cut out on traced line and use as a template so all 8 circles are uniform.

1. Using the template on page 85, cut 8 circles from tan wool or fabric of choice for penny circles.

2. Trace 8 circles onto fusible web. Cut out on the traced line, as shown.

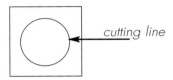

cutting line

3. Cut out the center of the fusible web leaving 1/2" on inside of circles traced line, as shown. This will eliminate stiffness when appliquéing through the layers.

cut out

4. Fuse the fusible web to the wrong side of the penny circles in step 1. Leave the paper on the fusible web.

Adding the Appliqués

1. Using the appliqué templates on pages 84-87, trace the shapes onto the paper side of the fusible web and cut out as directed.

2. Referring to the Basic Appliqué instructions on pages 10-11, prepare the fabric appliqué pieces. Referring to the layout guides on pages 84, 86, 87 and 91 position the appliqués and fuse in place.

3. Hand appliqué using a blanket stitch and the following thread colors:
   - Penny Circle and Small Center Star - #0178
   - Large Red Background Star - #78
   - Deer Head and Body, Moose Body, Small Tree Trunk and Pine Cones - #M90
   - Tall Tree Trunks, Moose Antlers, Snowshoes and Bear Nose - #0154
   - Skis, Log Cabin Roof and Cabin Logs - #P12
   - Ski Poles - Gray
   - Small Tree Branches, Large Tree Branches and Pine Branches - #0519
   - Snowshoe Poles - #1645
   - Bear Body - #1
   - Deer Antler and Words - Backstitch #P12

Finishing the Table Topper

1. Trace the circle freezer paper template onto fusible web. Cut out 1/4" beyond the traced line. Fuse to the wrong side of the black flannel backing fabric. When cool, peel fusible web paper from backing fabric. Reserve peeled paper for the next step.

2. Center the wool appliquéd top on the flannel backing wrong sides together. Place the reserved peeled paper on top of the appliquéd wool top. Fuse the pieces together using a steam iron and small presses. Be careful so the wool does not scorch. Trim away excess black flannel backing with sharp scissors.

3. Blanket stitch around the outside edge using black perle cotton.

Northern Exposure Penny Table Topper

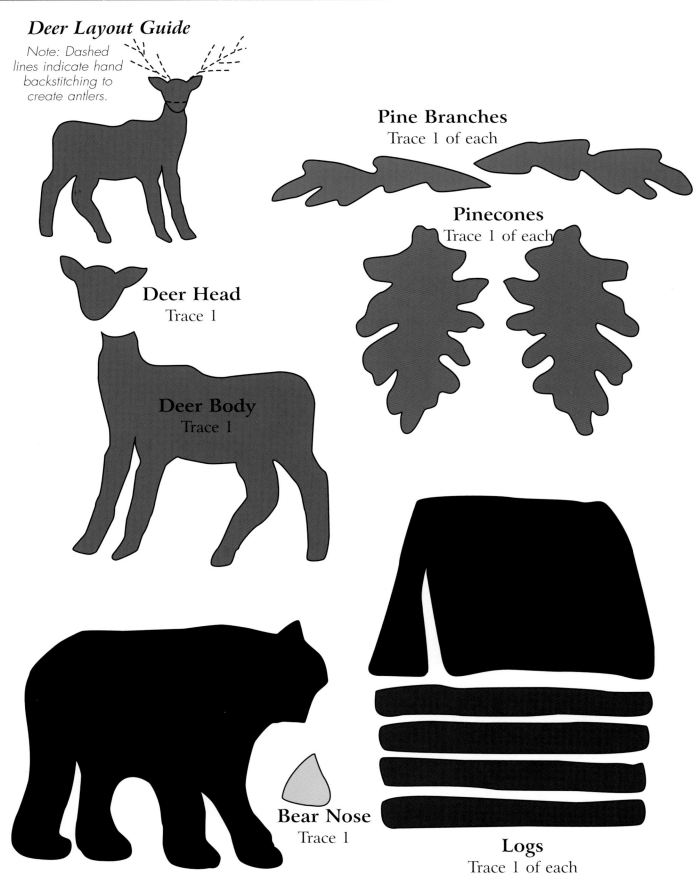

Deer Layout Guide

Note: Dashed lines indicate hand backstitching to create antlers.

Pine Branches
Trace 1 of each

Pinecones
Trace 1 of each

Deer Head
Trace 1

Deer Body
Trace 1

Bear Nose
Trace 1

Logs
Trace 1 of each

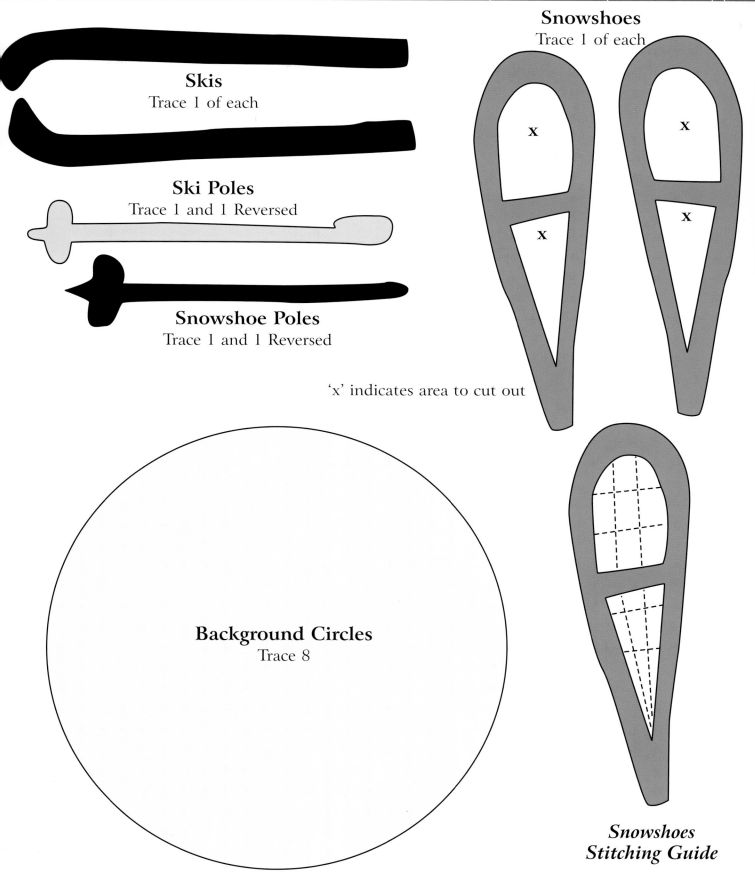

Skis
Trace 1 of each

Ski Poles
Trace 1 and 1 Reversed

Snowshoe Poles
Trace 1 and 1 Reversed

Snowshoes
Trace 1 of each

'x' indicates area to cut out

Background Circles
Trace 8

Snowshoes Stitching Guide

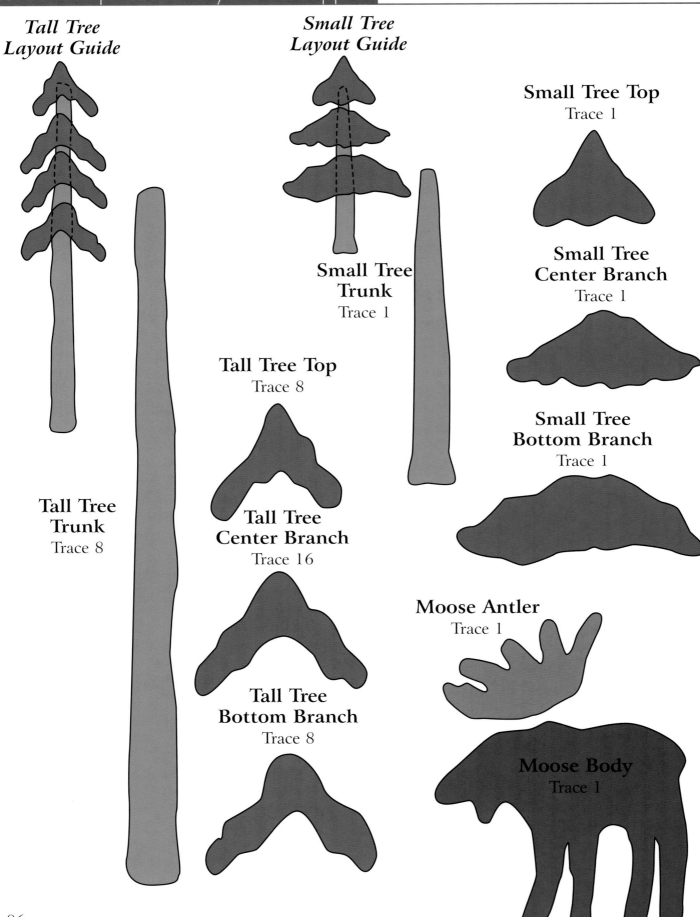

**Tall Tree
Layout Guide**

**Small Tree
Layout Guide**

Small Tree Top
Trace 1

**Small Tree
Center Branch**
Trace 1

**Small Tree
Trunk**
Trace 1

**Small Tree
Bottom Branch**
Trace 1

Tall Tree Top
Trace 8

**Tall Tree
Trunk**
Trace 8

**Tall Tree
Center Branch**
Trace 16

Moose Antler
Trace 1

**Tall Tree
Bottom Branch**
Trace 8

Moose Body
Trace 1

Note: Label tops of stars when tracing.

Top

Top

Large Star
Trace 1

Small Star
Trace 1

Every Day
is a
Blessing

(Embroidery Guide)

ornaments
northern exposure

Materials

Refer to the general instructions on pages 10-13 before starting this project.

Note: Project can be sewn in wool, flannel or cotton. Project shown is made using wool.

Ornaments can also be used as coasters.

8" x 12" piece of tan wool
for small penny circles

10-1/2" x 15" piece of red wool
for large background circles

1-1/2" x 2" piece of light brown wool
for pinecone

1-1/2" x 2" piece of light green wool
for pine branches

2" x 2-1/2" piece of brown wool
for moose body

1" x 2" piece of gold wool for moose antler

2" x 3" piece of dark brown wool
for log cabin roof

2" x 2-1/2" piece of medium brown wool
for cabin logs

2-1/2" x 3" piece of black wool
for bear body

1" x 1" square of light brown wool
for bear nose

2-1/2" x 3-1/2" piece of gold wool
for snowshoes

1-1/2" x 3" piece of dark brown wool
for snowshoe pole

1-1/2" x 3-1/2" piece of dark brown wool
for skis

1-1/2" x 3-1/2" piece of gray wool
for ski pole

18" x 22" piece of black flannel for backing

Lightweight paper-backed fusible web

Freezer paper

Valdani® Perle Cotton size 12 thread - #M90, #0519, #801, #154, #P12, #1, #1645, #0178, #78 and Gray

Jute, Ribbon or Leather Strip

Note: Yardage requirements are based on 44" wide unwashed flannel fabric. Please purchase accordingly if using prewashed, directional fabrics or felted wool. The wool fabrics in this project were prewashed.

instructions

Penny Circles Appliqués Background

*Helpful Hint: Trace the circle template onto a piece of cardboard or a plastic template sheet. Cut out on traced line and use as a template so all 6 circles are uniform.

1. Using the template on page 93, cut 6 circles from tan wool or fabric of choice for penny circles.

2. Trace 6 circles onto fusible web. Cut out on the traced line, as shown.

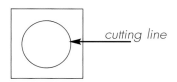

cutting line

3. Cut out the center of the fusible web leaving 1/2" on inside of circles traced line, as shown. This will eliminate stiffness when appliquéing through the layers.

cut out

4. Fuse the fusible web to the wrong side of the penny circles in step 1. Leave the paper on the fusible web.

Adding the Appliqués

1. Using the appliqué templates on pages 92-93, trace the shapes onto the paper side of the fusible web and cut out as directed.

2. Referring to the Basic Appliqué instructions on pages 10-11, prepare the fabric appliqué pieces. Referring to the layout guides on pages 91 and 93 position the appliqués and fuse them in place.

3. Hand appliqué using a blanket stitch and the following thread colors:
   - Pinecone - #M90
   - Pine Branch - #0519
   - Moose Body - #801
   - Moose Antler, Bear Nose and Snowshoes - #0154
   - Log Cabin Roof, Cabin Logs and Skis - #P12
   - Bear Body - #1
   - Snowshoe Poles - #1645
   - Ski Poles - Gray

Finishing the Ornaments

1. Trace the large circle template on page 93 onto a piece of cardboard or a plastic template sheet. Cut out on the traced line. Use this template so all 6 red wool circles are uniform.

2. Peel the paper from the back of the tan appliquéd circle and fuse to the red wool larger circle. Blanket stitch around outer edge of the center circle using #0178 perle cotton.

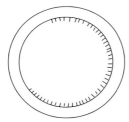

3. Trace the large circle template on page 93 onto fusible web. Cut out 1/4" beyond the traced line. Fuse to the wrong side of the black flannel backing fabric. When cooled, peel fusible web paper from black flannel backing. Reserve peeled paper for the next step.

4. Center the wool appliquéd circle on the flannel backing wrong sides together. Place the reserved peeled paper on top of the appliquéd wool ornament. Fuse the pieces together using a steam iron and small presses. Be careful so the wool does not scorch. Trim away excess black flannel backing with sharp scissors.

5. Blanket stitch around the outside edge using #78 perle cotton.

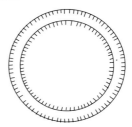

6. Cut a piece of jute, ribbon or leather strip 8" long. Make a loop for hanging and tack it at the top of the ornament. Cut another piece of jute, ribbon or leather strip 12-1/2" long and make a bow. Tack to the top of ornament. Three small jingle bells were tacked on the top of the bow.

Northern Exposure Ornaments
Layout Guides

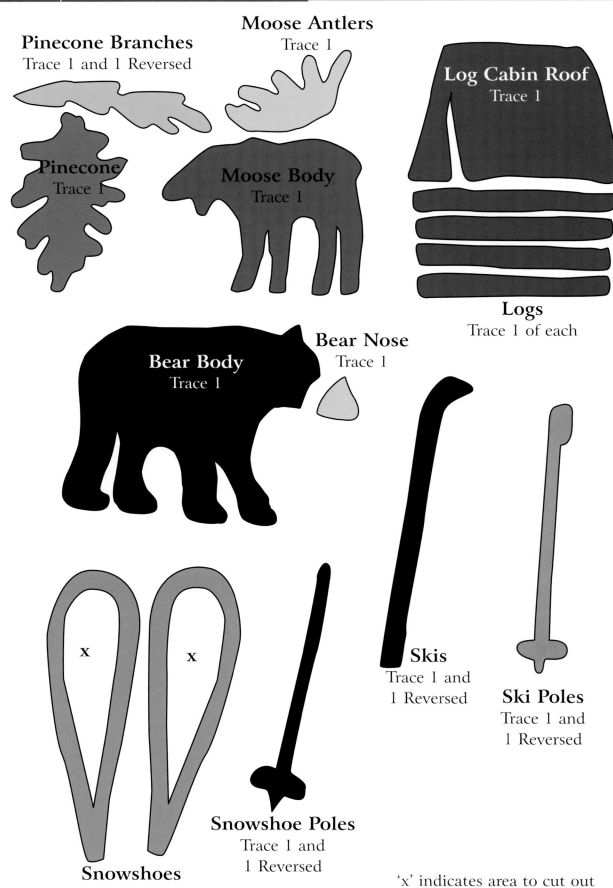

Pinecone Branches
Trace 1 and 1 Reversed

Moose Antlers
Trace 1

Log Cabin Roof
Trace 1

Pinecone
Trace 1

Moose Body
Trace 1

Logs
Trace 1 of each

Bear Body
Trace 1

Bear Nose
Trace 1

Skis
Trace 1 and
1 Reversed

Ski Poles
Trace 1 and
1 Reversed

x   x

Snowshoe Poles
Trace 1 and
1 Reversed

Snowshoes
Trace 1 of each

'x' indicates area to cut out

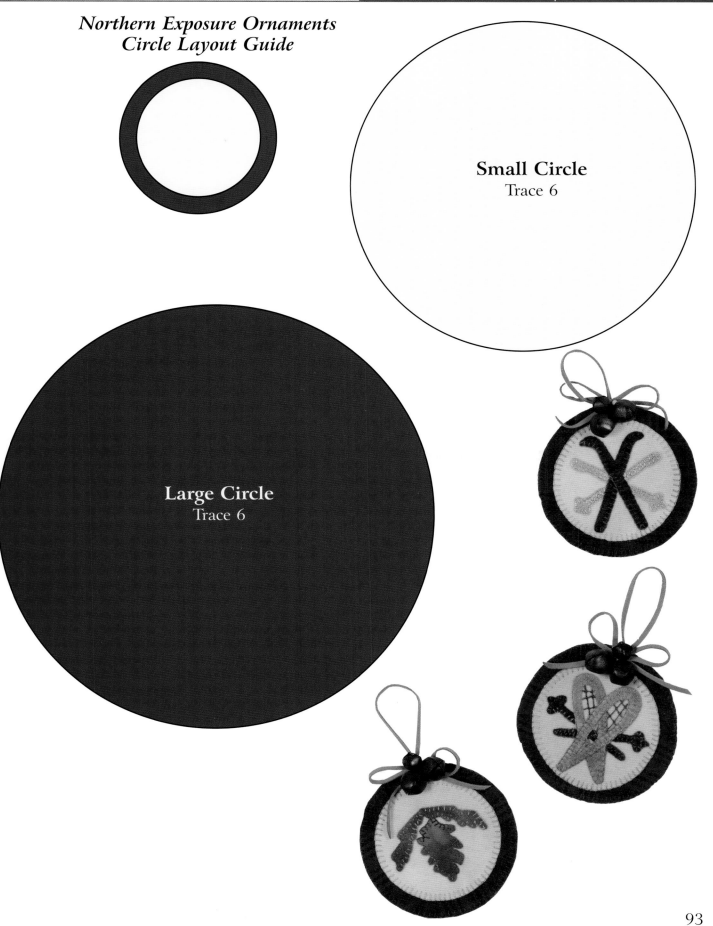

Northern Exposure Ornaments
Circle Layout Guide

Small Circle
Trace 6

Large Circle
Trace 6

end table topper
fishing and lodging

Finished size is approximately 9" x 16-1/2"

Materials

Refer to the general instructions on pages 10-13 before starting this project.

10" x 17-1/2" piece of light wool
for background

2-1/4" x 3-1/4" piece of gold plaid wool
for fish head

3" x 7" piece of brown plaid wool
for fish body

2" x 2-1/2" piece of brown stripe wool
for fish tail

3" x 4-1/2" piece of gold wool
for top fin and bottom fin

1-1/2" x 6" piece of dark brown wool
for tree trunks

2-1/4" x 7" piece of green wool
for tree branches

10-1/2" x 18" piece of flannel
for backing

Lightweight paper-backed fusible web

Freezer paper

Valdani® Perle Cotton size12 thread
#1645, #0519, #191, #1643,
#0154 and #PJ11

Note: Yardage requirements are based on 44" wide unwashed flannel fabric. Please purchase accordingly if using prewashed, directional fabrics or felted wool. Wool fabrics in this project were prewashed.

instructions

Making Oval Template

1. Fold an 11" x 17" piece of paper in half widthwise. The paper will measure approximately 8-1/2" x 11". Fold again lengthwise to create a double fold. Paper will measure approximately 5-1/2" x 8-1/2".

2. Trace the background template on page 98 on a piece of paper. Label folds and tracing/cutting line as indicated. Lay this template on the double folded paper, matching folds. Hold paper tightly on left fold side and cut out on cutting line. Unfold paper template.

 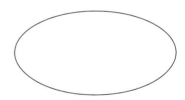

3. Lay the full size background template on the dull side of the freezer paper. Trace around the template and cut out 1/4" beyond the traced line.

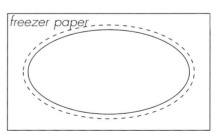

4. Place the freezer paper on the wrong side of the wool and iron. The freezer paper will adhere to the wool. Cut out the oval background on the traced line and remove freezer paper.

5. Trace the oval freezer paper template onto the fusible web. Cut out the center of the fusible web leaving approximately 1/2" along the outside edge. Fuse to the wool background oval. Do not remove the paper from the fusible web.

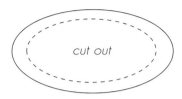

Adding the Appliqués

1. Using the appliqué templates on pages 96-97, trace the shapes onto the paper side of the fusible web and cut out as directed.

2. Referring to the Basic Appliqué instructions on pages 10-11, prepare the fabric appliqué pieces. Referring to the layout guide on page 97, position the appliqués and fuse them in place.

3. Hand appliqué using a blanket stitch and the following thread colors:
   • Tree Trunks, Fish Tail and Eye - #1645
   • Tree Branches - #0519
   • Fish Face - #191
   • Fish Body - #1643
   • Fish Fins - #0154
   • Words - Backstitch #1645

Finishing the End Table Topper

1. Peel the paper from the back of the appliquéd oval topper. Place on wrong side of flannel backing and fuse using a steam iron and small presses. Be careful not to scorch the wool. Trim away excess fabric with sharp scissors.

2. Blanket stitch the outside edge with #PJ11.

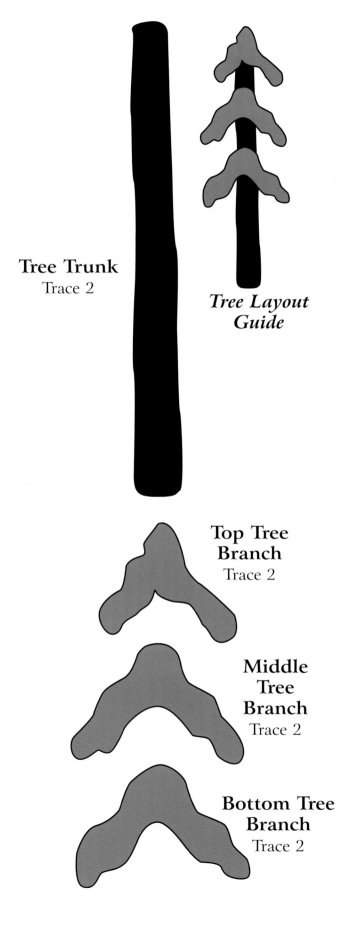

Tree Trunk
Trace 2

Tree Layout Guide

Top Tree Branch
Trace 2

Middle Tree Branch
Trace 2

Bottom Tree Branch
Trace 2

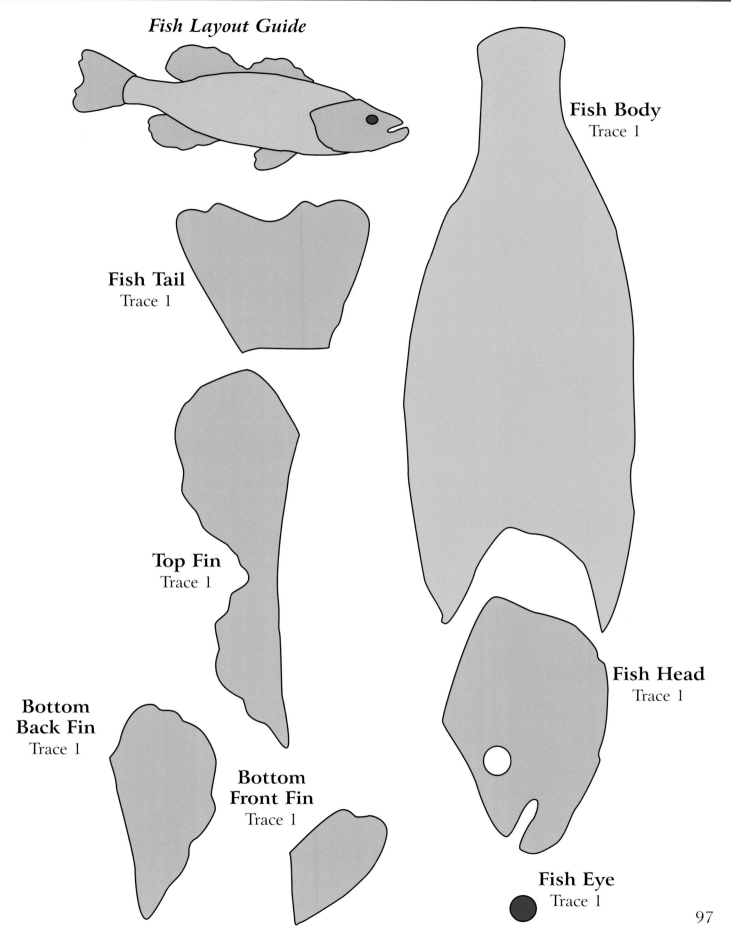

Fish Layout Guide

Fish Body
Trace 1

Fish Tail
Trace 1

Top Fin
Trace 1

Fish Head
Trace 1

Bottom Back Fin
Trace 1

Bottom Front Fin
Trace 1

Fish Eye
Trace 1

97

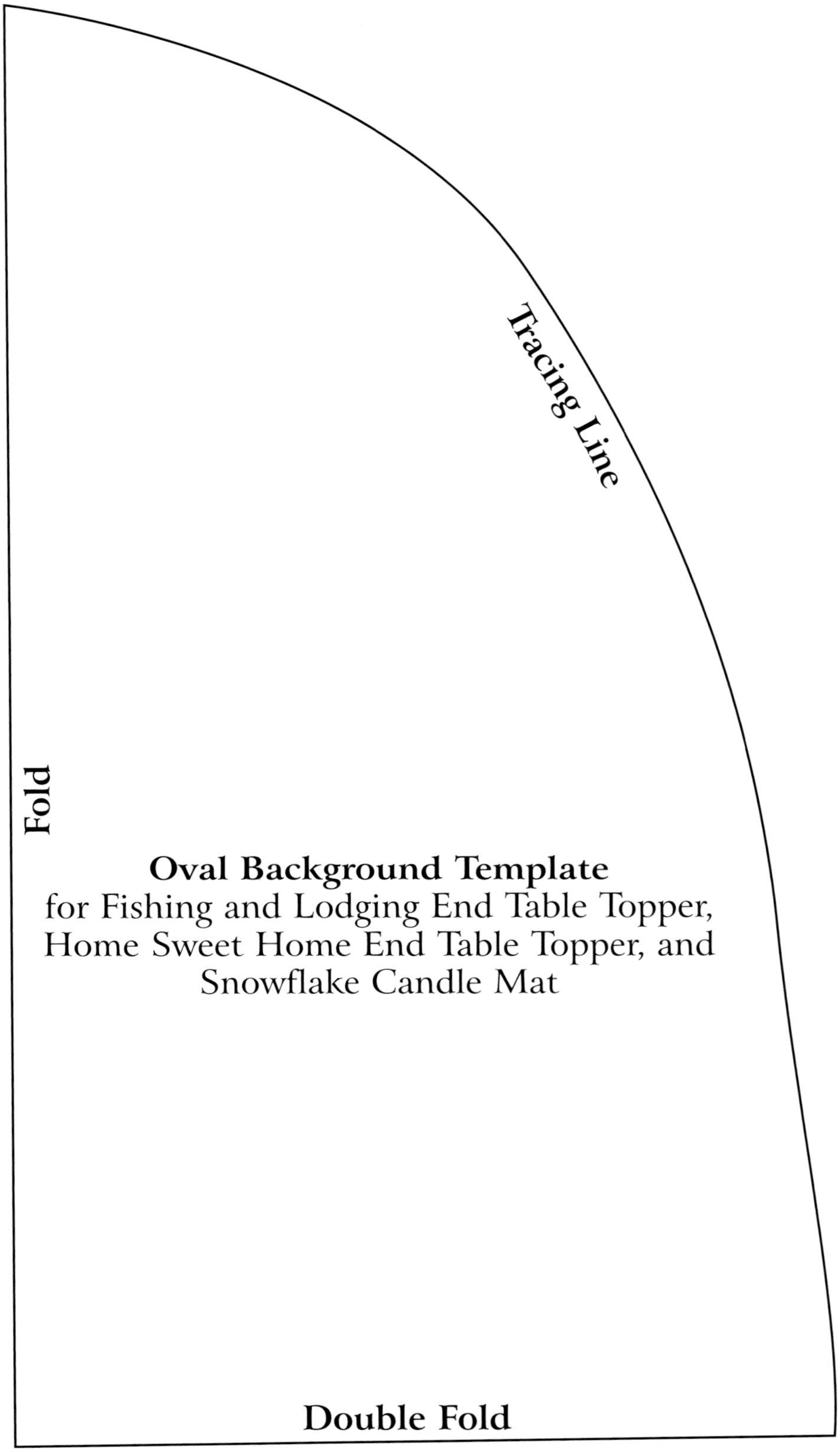

Tracing Line

Fold

Oval Background Template
for Fishing and Lodging End Table Topper,
Home Sweet Home End Table Topper, and
Snowflake Candle Mat

Double Fold

Fishing and Lodging

(Embroidery Guide)

Fishing and Lodging End Table Topper

end table topper
home sweet home

Finished size is approximately 9" x 16-1/2"

Materials

Refer to the general instructions on pages 10-13 before starting this project.

10" x 17-1/2" piece of light wool for background

1-1/4" x 5" piece of red wool for chimney

2-1/2" x 3-1/2" piece of black plaid wool for roof

2" x 3-1/2" piece of brown plaid wool for cabin logs

2-1/2" x 6" piece of rust wool for tree trunks

4-1/2" x 7-1/2" piece of green wool for tree branches

10-1/2" x 18" piece of flannel for backing

Lightweight paper-backed fusible web

Freezer paper

Valdani® Perle cotton size 12 thread - #191, #507, #1643, #1645 and #0576

Note: Yardage requirements are based on 44" wide unwashed flannel fabric. Please purchase accordingly if using prewashed, directional fabrics or felted wool. Wool fabrics in this project were prewashed.

Instructions

Making Oval Template

1. Fold an 11" x 17" piece of paper in half widthwise. The paper will measure approximately 8-1/2" x 11". Fold again lengthwise to create a double fold. Paper will measure approximately 5-1/2" x 8-1/2".

2. Trace the background template on page 98 on a piece of paper. Label folds and tracing/cutting line as indicated. Lay this template on the double folded paper, matching folds. Hold paper tightly on left fold side and cut out on cutting line. Unfold paper template.

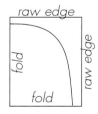 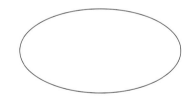

3. Lay the full size background template on the dull side of the freezer paper. Trace around the template and cut out 1/4" beyond the traced line.

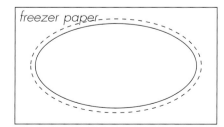

4. Place the freezer paper on the wrong side of the wool and iron. The freezer paper will adhere to the wool. Cut out the oval background on the traced line and remove freezer paper.

5. Trace the oval freezer paper template onto the fusible web. Cut out the center of the fusible web leaving approximately 1/2" along the outside edge. Fuse to the wool background oval. Do not remove the paper from the fusible web.

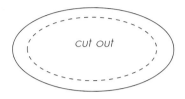

Adding the Appliqués

1. Using the appliqué templates on page 102, trace the shapes onto the paper side of the fusible web and cut out as directed.

2. Referring to the Basic Appliqué instructions on pages 10-11, prepare the fabric appliqué pieces. Referring to the layout guide on page 103, position the appliqués and fuse them in place.

3. Hand appliqué using a blanket stitch and the following thread colors:
   - Chimney - #0507
   - Tree Branches - #191
   - Tree Trunks and Cabin Bottom - #1643
   - Cabin Roof - #1645
   - Words - Backstitch #1643

Finishing the End Table Topper

1. Peel the paper from the back of the appliquéd oval topper. Place on wrong side of flannel backing and fuse using a steam iron and small presses. Be careful not to scorch the wool. Trim away excess fabric with sharp scissors.

2. Blanket stitch the outside edge with #0576.

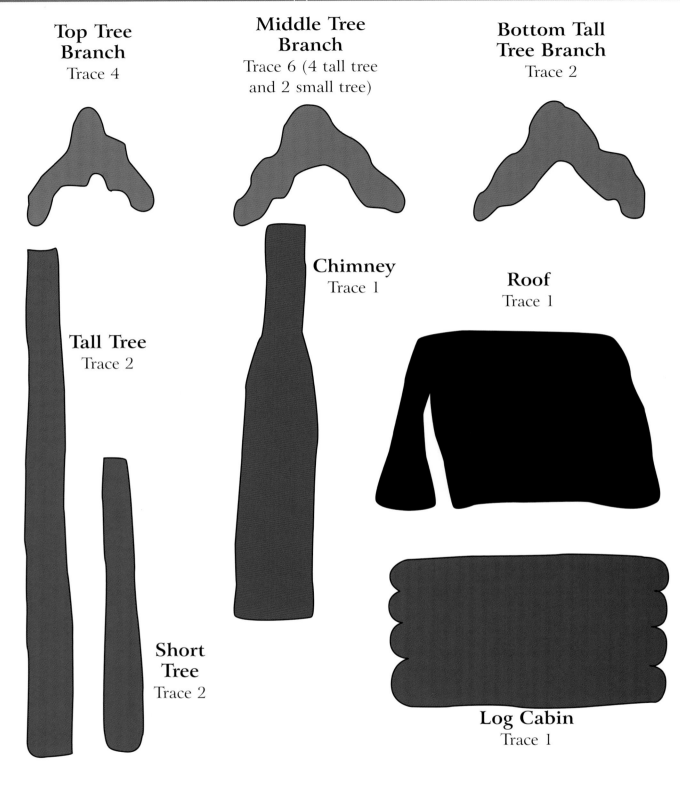

**Top Tree
Branch**
Trace 4

**Middle Tree
Branch**
Trace 6 (4 tall tree
and 2 small tree)

**Bottom Tall
Tree Branch**
Trace 2

Tall Tree
Trace 2

Chimney
Trace 1

Roof
Trace 1

**Short
Tree**
Trace 2

Log Cabin
Trace 1

Home Sweet Home
(Embroidery Guide)

Home Sweet Home End Table Topper Layout Guide

candle mat
snowflake

Finished size is approximately 9" x 16–1/2"

Materials

Refer to the general instructions on pages 10-13 before starting this project.

10" x 17-1/2" piece of teal wool
for background

7-1/2" x 7-1/2" square of white wool
for large snowflake

4-1/2" x 8-1/2" piece of white wool
for small snowflake

11" x 19" piece of flannel for backing

Lightweight paper-backed fusible web

Freezer paper

Valdani® Perle Cotton
size 12 thread - #H203

DMC® Perle Cotton
size 8 thread - #712

*Note: Yardage requirements are based on
44" wide unwashed flannel fabric. Please
purchase accordingly if using prewashed,
directional fabrics or felted wool. Wool fabrics in
this project were prewashed.*

Instructions

Making Oval Template

1. Fold an 11" x 17" piece of paper in half widthwise. The paper will measure approximately 8-1/2" x 11". Fold again lengthwise to create a double fold. Paper will measure approximately 5-1/2" x 8-1/2".

 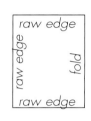 

2. Trace the background template on page 98 on a piece of paper. Label folds and tracing/cutting line as indicated. Lay this template on the double folded paper, matching folds. Hold paper tightly on left fold side and cut out on cutting line. Unfold paper template.

 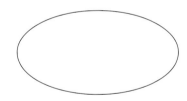

3. Lay the full size background template on the dull side of the freezer paper. Trace around the template and cut out 1/4" beyond the traced line.

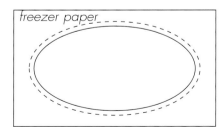

4. Place the freezer paper on the wrong side of the wool and iron. The freezer paper will adhere to the wool. Cut out the oval background on the traced line and remove freezer paper.

5. Trace the oval freezer paper template onto the fusible web. Cut out the center of the fusible web leaving approximately 1/2" along the outside edge. Fuse to the wool background oval. Do not remove the paper from the fusible web.

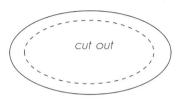

Adding the Appliqués

1. Using the appliqué templates on pages 106-107, trace the shapes onto the paper side of the fusible web and cut out as directed.

2. Referring to the Basic Appliqué instructions on pages 10-11, prepare the fabric appliqué pieces. Referring to the layout guide on page 107, position and fuse the appliqués in place.

3. Hand appliqué using a blanket stitch and the following thread color:
   • Snowflakes - #712

Finishing the Candle Mat

1. Peel the paper from the back of appliquéd oval candle mat. Place on wrong side of flannel backing and fuse using a steam iron and small presses. Be careful not to scorch the wool. Trim away excess fabric with sharp scissors.

2. Blanket stitch the outside edge with #H203.

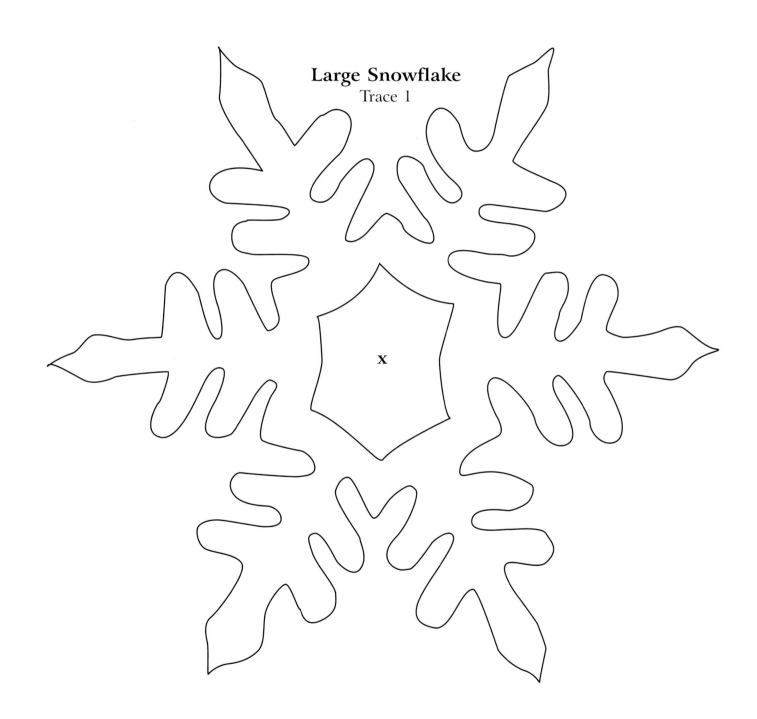

Large Snowflake
Trace 1

x

'x' indicates area to cut out

Small Snowflake
Trace 2

Snowflake Candle Mat Layout Guide

place mat
cherry orchard

Finished size is approximately 13" x 19"

Materials

Refer to the general instructions on pages 10-13 before starting this project.

Yardage given will make 1 place mat

1/6 yard of lemon freeze marblecake fabric
for appliqué background

2/3 yard of cherry print fabric for front and back

1/4 yard of cucumber marblecake fabric
for binding

1" x 3" piece of green marblecake fabric
for leaves

1-1/2" x 3-1/2" piece of
red marblecake fabric for cherries

17" x 21" piece of batting

Lightweight paper-backed fusible web

Lightweight tear-away stabilizer

Sulky® thread to match appliqués

*Note: Fabrics are based on 44"-wide fabrics that
have not been washed. Please purchase accordingly
if using prewashed or directional fabrics.*

Instructions

Cutting

From lemon freeze marblecake fabric:
  Cut 1 strip — 4" x 44";
    from strip cut 1 — 4" x 4" square.

From cherry print fabric:
  Cut piece in half lengthwise for 2 pieces approximately 22" x 27". Reserve 1 piece for the backing.
  Cut 1 — 8-3/4" x 19-1/2" rectangle.
  Cut 1 — 5-1/4" x 14-3/4" rectangle.
  Cut 1 — 1-3/4" x 5-1/4" rectangle.
  Cut 1 — 1-3/4" x 4" rectangle.

From cucumber marblecake fabric:
  Cut 2 strips — 2-1/2" x 44".

Adding the Appliqués

1. Using the appliqué templates below, trace the shapes onto the paper side of the fusible web and cut out as directed.

2. Referring to the Basic Appliqué instructions on pages 10-11, prepare the fabric appliqué pieces. Referring to the photograph on page 108, position and fuse the appliqués in place.

3. Use a small zigzag stitch and matching thread to appliqué each shape to the place mat. Remember to use tear-away stabilizer when stitching appliqués.

Place Mat Assembly

1. Sew together the cherry print 1-3/4" x 4" rectangle and the lemon freeze marblecake 4" x 4" square, as shown. Press seam allowances toward the dark fabric. Make 1 Unit A.

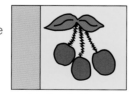

Make 1 Unit A

2. Sew the cherry print 1-3/4" x 5-1/4" rectangle to Unit A, as shown. Press seam allowances toward the dark fabric. Make 1 Unit B.

Make 1 Unit B

3. Sew the cherry print 5-1/4" x 14-3/4" rectangle to Unit B, as shown. Press seam allowances toward the dark fabric. Make 1 Unit C.

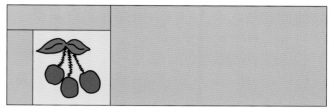

Make 1 Unit C

4. Sew the cherry print 8-3/4" x 19-1/2" rectangle to Unit C, as shown. Press seam allowances toward the dark fabric.

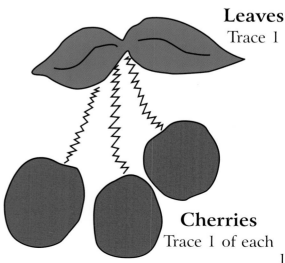

Finishing the Place Mat

Layer the backing fabric, batting and place mat top. Baste the layers together. Hand or machine quilt as desired. Finish the place mat by sewing binding to the edges following the steps in Basic Binding on page 12.

Leaves
Trace 1

Cherries
Trace 1 of each

place mat
dragonfly summer

Finished size is approximately 13" x 19"

Materials

Refer to the general instructions on pages 10-13 before starting this project.

Yardage given will make 1 place mat

1/6 yard of lemon freeze marblecake fabric for appliqué background

2/3 yard of yellow marblecake fabric for front and back

1/4 yard of green woodgrain fabric for binding

6" x 7" piece of gold marblecake fabric for flower

2" x 2" square of chocolate marblecake fabric for flower center

11" x 13" piece of green woodgrain for flower stem

1-1/2" x 2-1/2" piece of brown woodgrain for dragonfly body

2-1/2" x 3-1/2" piece of teal woodgrain for dragonfly wings

17" x 21" piece of batting

Lightweight paper-backed fusible web

Lightweight tear-away stabilizer

Sulky® thread to match appliqués

Note: Fabrics are based on 44"-wide fabrics that have not been washed. Please purchase accordingly if using prewashed or directional fabrics.

instructions

Cutting

From lemon freeze marblecake fabric:
  Cut 1 strip — 4" x 44";
    from strip cut 1 — 4" x 4" square.

From yellow marblecake fabric:
  Cut piece in half lengthwise for 2 pieces approximately 22" x 27". Reserve 1 piece for the backing.
  Cut 1 — 8-3/4" x 19-1/2" rectangle.
  Cut 1 — 5-1/4" x 14-3/4" rectangle.
  Cut 1 — 1-3/4" x 5-1/4" rectangle.
  Cut 1 — 1-3/4" x 4" rectangle.

From green woodgrain fabric:
  Cut 2 strips — 2-1/2" x 44".

Adding the Appliqués

1. Using the appliqué templates on page 113, trace the shapes onto the paper side of the fusible web and cut out as directed.

2. Referring to the Basic Appliqué instructions on pages 10-11, prepare the fabric appliqué pieces. Referring to the layout guides on pages 112-113, position and fuse the appliqués in place.

3. Use a small zigzag stitch and matching thread to appliqué each shape to the place mat. Remember to use tear-away stabilizer when stitching appliqués.

Place Mat Assembly

1. Sew together the yellow marblecake 1-3/4" x 4" rectangle and the lemon freeze marblecake 4" x 4" square, as shown. Press seam allowances toward the dark fabric. Make 1 Unit A.

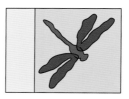

Make 1 Unit A

2. Sew the yellow marblecake 1-3/4" x 5-1/4" rectangle to Unit A, as shown. Press seam allowances toward the dark fabric. Make 1 Unit B.

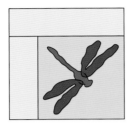

Make 1 Unit B

3. Sew the yellow marblecake 5-1/4" x 14-3/4" rectangle to Unit B, as shown. Press seam allowances toward the dark fabric. Make 1 Unit C.

Make 1 Unit C

4. Sew the yellow marblecake 8-3/4" x 19-1/2" rectangle to Unit C, as shown. Press seam allowances toward the dark fabric.

Finishing the Place Mat

Layer the backing fabric, batting and place mat top. Baste the layers together. Hand or machine quilt as desired. Finish the place mat by sewing binding to the edges following the steps in Basic Binding on page 12.

Dragonfly Summer Place Mat Layout Guide

Dragonfly Layout Diagram

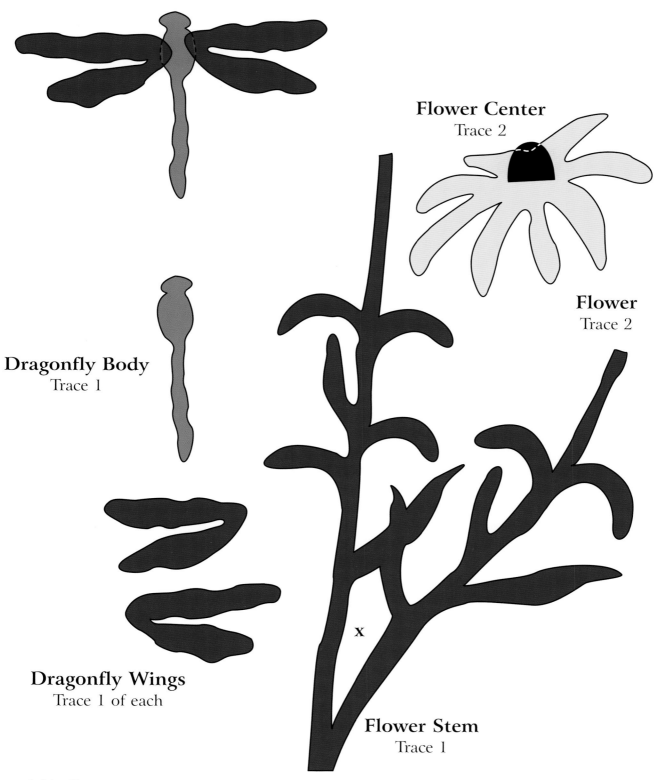

Flower Center
Trace 2

Flower
Trace 2

Dragonfly Body
Trace 1

Dragonfly Wings
Trace 1 of each

x

Flower Stem
Trace 1

'x' indicates area to cut out

place mat
pheasant

Finished size is approximately 13" x 19"

Materials

Refer to the general instructions on pages 10-13 before starting this project.

Yardage given will make 1 place mat

1 yard of gold pheasant feathers
fabric for front, back and binding

1/6 yard of pheasant print fabric for front

17" x 21" piece of batting

*Note: Fabrics are based on 44"-wide fabrics
that have not been washed. Please purchase
accordingly if using prewashed or directional fabrics.*

Instructions

Cutting

From gold pheasant feather fabric:

Cut 2 strips — 2-1/2" x 44".

Cut remaining piece in half lengthwise for 2 pieces approximately 22" x 27".

Reserve 1 piece for the backing.

Cut 1 — 8-3/4" x 19-1/2" rectangle.

Cut 1 — 5-1/4" x 14-3/4" rectangle.

Cut 1 — 1-3/4" x 5-1/4" rectangle.

Cut 1 — 1-3/4" x 4" rectangle.

From pheasant print fabric:

Fussy cut 1 — 4" x 4" square.

Place Mat Assembly

1. Sew together the gold pheasant feather 1-3/4" x 4" rectangle and the pheasant print 4" x 4" square, as shown. Press seam allowances toward the dark fabric. Make 1 Unit A.

Make 1 Unit A

2. Sew the gold pheasant feather 1-3/4" x 5-1/4" rectangle to Unit A, as shown. Press seam allowances toward the dark fabric. Make 1 Unit B.

Make 1 Unit B

3. Sew the gold pheasant feather 5-1/4" x 14-3/4" rectangle to Unit B, as shown. Press seam allowances toward the dark fabric. Make 1 Unit C.

Make 1 Unit C

4. Sew the gold pheasant feather 8-3/4" x 19-1/2" rectangle to Unit C, as shown. Press seam allowances toward the dark fabric.

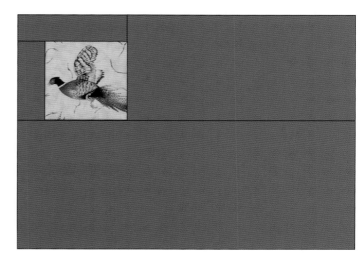

Finishing the Place Mat

Layer the backing fabric, batting and place mat top. Baste the layers together. Hand or machine quilt as desired. Finish the place mat by sewing binding to the edges following the steps in Basic Binding on page 12.

table runner
tree of life friendship

Forever true, forever friends.

Materials

Refer to the general instructions on pages 10-13 before starting this project.

1/8 yard of olive woodgrain fabric for tree block triangles

1/8 yard of teal woodgrain fabric for tree block triangles

1/8 yard of olive marblecake fabric for tree block triangles

1/8 yard of olive fabric for tree block triangles

1/8 yard of dark green marblecake fabric for tree block triangles

5/8 yard of tan marblecake fabric for tree block background and signature block

1/4 yard of dark olive marblecake fabric for tree block triangles

1/4 yard of red marblecake fabric for signature block

1/4 yard of golden brown woodgrain fabric for sashing and inner border

1 yard of blue background trees fabric for outer border and binding

1-1/4" x 3-1/2" piece of golden brown woodgrain fabric for tree trunk

1-3/8 yards of backing fabric

25" x 46" piece of batting

Lightweight paper-backed fusible web

Lightweight tear-away stabilizer

Note: Fabrics are based on 44"-wide fabrics that have not been washed. Please purchase accordingly if using prewashed or directional fabrics.

The inspiration for this table runner is close to my heart. I moved away from lifelong friends a few years ago and at our last sewing group night, I received a very cherished gift— a wallhanging signed by all my stitching friends. It now hangs in my new sewing room and brings back so many wonderful memories of the good times we shared. My pals still get together every Thursday for coffee and quilt talk.

It inspired me to include a signature table runner for friends and family to sign to commemorate special occassions—Mom and Dad's wedding anniversary, grandma or grandpa's birthday celebration or even a family reunion. The runner can also be sewn in cream tones for wedding guests to sign.

What fun memories! Tree of Life, after all that's what life's all about, family and friends.

Debbie

Note: After the center becomes full of signatures, sign around the pieced trees or even on the back of the runner.

Instructions

Cutting

From olive woodgrain fabric:
Cut 1 strip — 2-1/8" x 44";
from strip cut 3 — 2-1/8" x 2-1/8" squares.
Cut squares in half diagonally to make 6 half-square triangles.

From teal woodgrain fabric:
Cut 1 strip — 2-1/8" x 44";
from strip cut 3 — 2-1/8" x 2-1/8" squares.
Cut squares in half diagonally to make 6 half-square triangles.

From olive marblecake fabric:
Cut 1 strip — 2-1/8" x 44";
from the strip cut 2 — 2-1/8" x 2-1/8" squares.
Cut squares in half diagonally to make 4 half-square triangles.

From olive fabric:
Cut 1 strip — 2-1/8" x 44";
from strip cut 3 — 2-1/8" x 2-1/8" squares.
Cut squares in half diagonally to make 6 half-square triangles.

From dark green marblecake fabric:
Cut 1 strip — 2-1/8" x 44";
from strip cut 3 — 2-1/8" x 2-1/8" squares.
Cut squares in half diagonally to make 6 half-square triangles.

From tan marblecake fabric:
Cut 1 strip — 2-1/8" x 44";
from strip cut 14 — 2-1/8" x 2-1/8" squares.
Cut squares in half diagonally to make 28 half-square triangles.
Cut 1 strip — 5-3/4" x 44";
from strip cut 4 — 5-3/4" x 5-3/4" squares.
Cut squares in half diagonally to make 8 half-square triangles.
Cut 1 strip — 4-5/8" x 44";
from strip cut 1 — 4-5/8" x 4-5/8" square.
Cut square in half diagonally to make 2 half-square triangles.

Cut 1 strip — 1-3/4" x 44";
from strip cut 4 — 1-3/4" x 1-3/4" squares.
Cut 1 strip — 2-3/4" x 44";
from strip cut 8 — 2-3/4" x 5" rectangles.

From dark olive marblecake fabric:
Cut 1 strip — 4-5/8" x 44";
from strip cut 1 — 4-5/8" x 4-5/8" square.
Cut square in half diagonally to make 2 half-square triangles.

From red marblecake fabric:
Cut 2 strips — 2-3/4" x 44";
from strip cut 16 — 2-3/4" x 2-3/4" squares.

From golden brown woodgrain fabric:
Cut 3 strips — 2" x 44";
from 1 strip cut 4 — 2" x 9-1/2" rectangles.

From blue background trees fabric:
Cut 1 strip — 14" x 44";
from strip cut 2 — 3-1/2" x 14" rectangles.
Cut 2 strips — 3-1/2" x 44".
Cut 3 strips — 2-3/4" x 44".

Adding the Appliqué

1. Using the appliqué template below, trace the shapes onto the paper side of the fusible web and cut out as directed.

2. Referring to the Basic Appliqué instructions on pages 10-11, prepare the fabric appliqué pieces. Referring to the photograph on page 116, position the 1/2" x 3-1/2" golden brown woodgrain tree trunk to the tan marblecake 4-5/8" half-square triangle and fuse in place.

3. Use a small zigzag stitch and matching thread to appliqué shape to the triangle. Remember to use tear-away stabilizer when stitching appliqués.

Tree Trunk
Trace 2

Tree Block Assembly

1. Sew together the appliquéd tan marblecake 4-5/8" half-square triangle and dark olive marblecake 4-5/8" half-square triangle, as shown. Press seam allowances toward the dark fabric. Repeat to make 2 Unit A.

Make 2 Unit A

2. Arrange the assorted green 2-1/8" half-square triangles in a pleasing manner.

3. Sew together a green and tan marblecake 2-1/8" half-square triangle, as shown. Press seam allowances toward the dark fabric. Repeat to make 14 Unit B.

Make 14 Unit B

4. Sew together a green and tan marblecake 2-1/8" half-square triangle, as shown. Press seam allowances toward the dark fabric. Repeat to make 14 Unit C.

Make 14 Unit C

5. Sew 3 Unit B together, as shown. Press seam allowances open. Repeat to make 2 Unit D.

Make 2 Unit D

6. Sew 4 Unit B together, as shown. Press seam allowances open. Repeat to make 2 Unit E.

Make 2 Unit E

7. Sew 3 Unit C together, as shown. Press seam allowances open. Repeat to make 2 Unit F.

Make 2 Unit F

8. Sew 4 Unit C together, as shown. Press seam allowances open. Repeat to make 2 Unit G.

Make 2 Unit G

9. Sew a Unit D to a Unit A, as shown. Press seam allowances open. Repeat to make 2 Unit H.

Make 2 Unit H

10. Sew a tan marblecake 1-3/4" square to a Unit F, as shown. Press seam allowances open. Repeat to make 2 Unit I.

Make 2 Unit I

11. Sew a Unit I to a Unit H, as shown. Press seam allowances open. Repeat to make 2 Unit J.

Make 2 Unit J

12. Sew a Unit E to a Unit J, as shown. Press seam allowances open. Repeat to make 2 Unit K.

Make 2 Unit K

13. Sew a tan marblecake 1-3/4" square to a Unit G, as shown. Press seam allowances open. Repeat to make 2 Unit L.

Make 2 Unit L

14. Sew a Unit L to a Unit K, as shown. Press seam allowances open. Repeat to make 2 tree blocks.

Make 2 Tree Blocks

15. Sew a tan marblecake 5-3/4" half-square triangle to each side of the tree block. Press seam allowances toward the outside. Repeat to make 2 tree blocks.

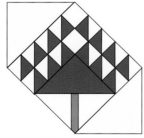

Make 2 Tree Blocks

16. Sew a tan marblecake 5-3/4" half-square triangle to the remaining sides of the tree block. Press seam allowances toward the outside. Repeat to make 2 tree blocks.

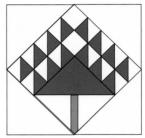

Make 2 Tree Blocks

17. Square up the blocks to measure 9-1/2". Be sure to leave a 1/4" beyond the seam intersections.

Signature Block Assembly

1. Draw a diagonal line on the back of the red marble 2-3/4" x 2-3/4" squares.

2. Place a red marblecake 2-3/4" square on a tan marblecake 2-3/4" x 5" rectangle. Sew on the diagonal line. Press the red marblecake square toward the outside. Trim away the center red marblecake triangle only. Repeat to make 8 Unit A.

Make 8 Unit A

3. Place a red marblecake 2-3/4" square on the opposite corner of the tan marblecake 2-3/4" x 5" rectangle. Sew on the diagonal line. Press the red marblecake square toward the

outside. Trim away the center red marblecake triangle only. Repeat to make 8 Unit B.

Make 8 Unit B

4. Sew 4 Unit B together, as shown, to make 1 row. Press the seam allowances open. Repeat to make 2 rows.

Make 2 Rows

5. Sew the 2 rows together, as shown, to make 1 Signature Block. Press the seam allowances open.

Make 1 Signature Block

Table Runner Assembly

1. Sew the 2 tree blocks, 1 signature block and the 4 golden brown woodgrain 2" x 9-1/2" sashing strips together, as shown. Press seam allowances toward the sashing.

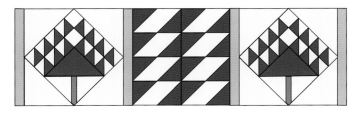

2. Measure the width of the table runner through the center for the top and bottom border measurement. Use this measurement to cut two lengths from the 2"-wide golden brown woodgrain strips. Sew the lengths to the top and bottom edges of the table

runner. Press seam allowances toward the dark fabric.

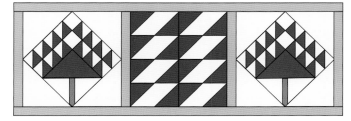

3. Measure the length of the table runner top through the center to determine the side border measurement. Cut 2 strips from the blue background trees 3-1/2" x 14" rectangles to the length needed. Sew the strips to each side of the runner. Press seam allowances toward the border.

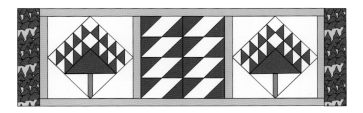

4. Measure the width of the runner top through the center for top and bottom border measurement. Use this measurement to cut 2 strips from the blue background trees 3-1/2"-wide strips. Sew the strips to the top and bottom of the runner. Press seam allowances toward the border.

Finishing the Table Runner

Layer the backing fabric, batting and table runner top. Baste the layers together. Hand or machine quilt as desired. Finish the table runner by sewing binding to the edges following the steps in Basic Binding on page 12.

121

table runner
summer fishing

Finished size is approximately 18" x 48"

Materials

Refer to the general instructions on pages 10-13 before starting this project.

1/2 yard of ecru background lures fabric for block background

1/2 yard of gold texture fabric for sashing and inner border

1-1/4 yards of blue background fish fabric for blocks, outer border and binding

1-1/2 yards of backing fabric

23" x 53" piece of batting

Note: Fabrics are based on 44"-wide fabrics that have not been washed. Please purchase accordingly if using prewashed or directional fabrics.

instructions

Cutting

From ecru background lures fabric:
  Cut 4 strips — 3-1/2" x 44";
    from strip cut 48 — 3-1/2" x 3-1/2" squares.

From gold texture fabric:
  Cut 5 strips — 2-1/2" x 44";
    from 2 strips cut 4 — 2-1/2" x 12-1/2" rectangles.

From blue background fish fabric:
  Cut 4 strips — 3-1/2" x 44";
    from strip cut 24 — 3-1/2" x 6-1/2" rectangles.
  Cut 4 strips — 4" x 44".
  Cut 4 strips — 2-3/4" x 44".

Block Assembly

1. Draw a diagonal line on the wrong side of each 3-1/2" ecru background lure square, as shown.

2. Place an ecru background lure 3-1/2" square on a blue background fish 3-1/2" x 6-1/2" rectangle. Sew on the diagonal line, as shown. Press the triangle toward the outside edge. Trim away the middle triangle only. Repeat to make 24 Unit A.

Make 24 Unit A

3. Sew an ecru background lure 3-1/2" square on the opposite end of a Unit A. Sew on the diagonal line. Press the triangle toward the outside edge. Trim away the middle triangle only. Repeat to make 24 Unit B.

Make 24 Unit B

4. Sew 2 Unit B together, as shown. Press the seam allowances open. Repeat to make 12 Unit C.

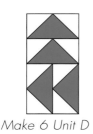

Make 12 Unit C

5. Sew 2 Unit C together, as shown. Press the seam allowances open. Repeat to make 6 Unit D.

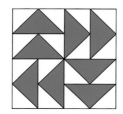

Make 6 Unit D

6. Sew 2 Unit D together, as shown. Press the seam allowances open. Repeat to make 3 Unit E.

Make 3 Unit E

Table Runner Assembly

1. Sew the 3 Unit E and the 4 gold texture 2-1/2" x 12-1/2" sashing strips together, as shown. Press seam allowances toward the dark fabric.

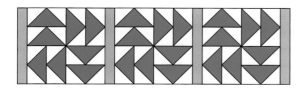

2. Measure the width of the table runner through the center for the top and bottom border measurement. Use this measurement to cut two lengths from the 2-1/2"-wide gold texture strips.

Sew the lengths to the top and bottom edges of the table runner. Press seam allowances toward the dark fabric.

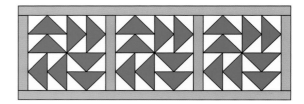

3. Measure the length of the table runner top through the center to determine the side border measurement. Cut 2, 4"-wide strips from the blue background fish to the length needed. Sew the strips to each side of the runner. Press seam allowances toward the dark fabric.

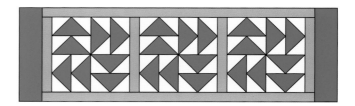

4. Measure the width of the runner top through the center for top and bottom border measurement. Use this measurement to cut 2 strips from the blue background fish 4"-wide strips. Sew the strips to the top and bottom of the runner. Press seam allowances toward the dark fabric.

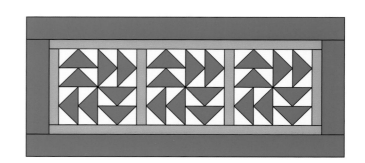

Finishing the Table Runner

Layer the backing fabric, batting and table runner top. Baste the layers together. Hand or machine quilt as desired. Finish the table runner by sewing binding to the edges following the steps in Basic Binding on page 12.

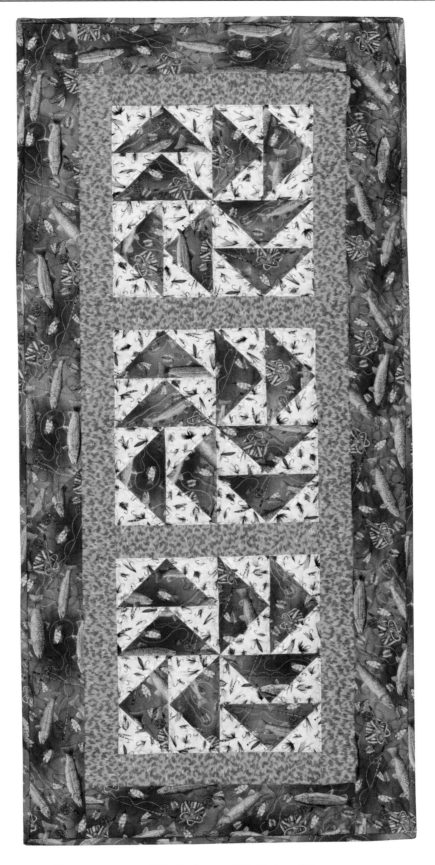

Summer Fishing Table Runner

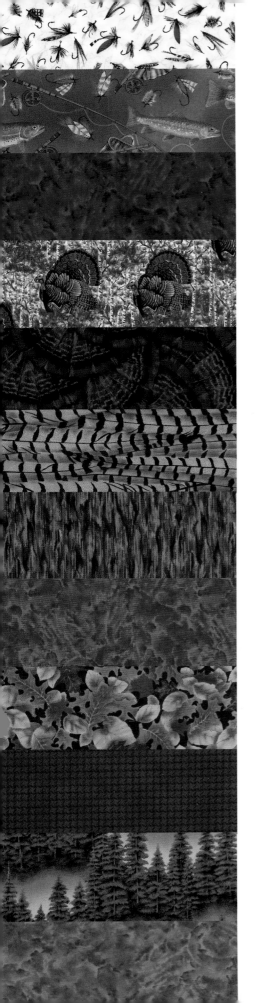

Visit your local quilt shop and ask for
Granola Girl® Designs fabrics
manufactured by Troy Corporation, or
visit www.granolagirldesigns.com.

Fabric collections used to make the cotton projects
in this book include:
Marblecake Basics, Sport Fishing, Gone Fishing and
Pheasant and Turkey Season

Embroidery threads used for machine appliqué are
40 wt rayon and available from Sulky® of America, Inc.
Visit www.sulky.com